SAM BARTRAM

The Story of a Goalkeeping Legend

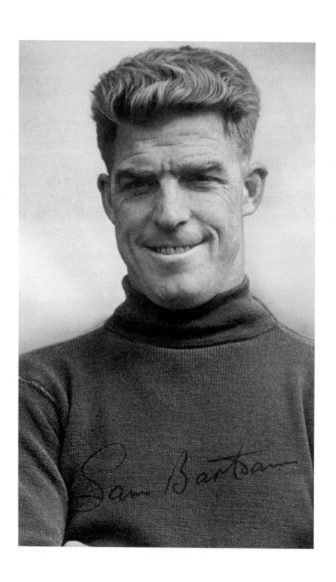

SAM
The Story of a
Goalkeeping Legend
BARTRAM

Mike Blake

TEMPUS

*To my father who took me to see Sam Bartram play, my mother who knitted
me a goalkeeper's sweater so I could look like Sam Bartram, Moira Bartram for
all her help and to those who so eagerly contributed*

Cover Photo: Sam Bartram leads out Charlton on his 800th and
final appearance in March 1956. *(Empics)*

First published 2006

Tempus Publishing Limited
The Mill, Brimscombe Port,
Stroud, Gloucestershire, GL5 2QG
www.tempus-publishing.com

© Mike Blake, 2006

The right of Mike Blake to be identified as the Author
of this work has been asserted in accordance with the
Copyrights, Designs and Patents Act 1988.

British Library Cataloguing in Publication Data.
A catalogue record for this book is available from the British Library.

ISBN 0 7524 3574 4

Typesetting and origination by Tempus Publishing Limited
Printed in Great Britain

CONTENTS

PHOTOGRAPHIC ACKNOWLEDGEMENTS

Page 12 By permission of Durham County Record Office, D/X 148/11, D/X 148/21, D/X 148/19; Page 13 DRO D/X 148/20; Page 15 (top left and centre) South Tyneside Library; Page 17 Sam Bartram Collection; Page 18 British Library Newspapers; Page 19 British Library Newspapers; Page 22 Bartram family collection; Page 23 Bartram family collection; Page 24 Bartram family collection; Page 25 Bartram family collection; Page 30 (top) Empics; Page 31 Bartram family collection; Page 32 (left) Bartram family collection; Page 33 Bartram family collection; Page 34 Bartram family collection; Page 35 Bartram family collection; Page 36 Sam Bartram Collection; Page 38 Bartram family collection; Page 39 (top) Bartram family collection (bottom left and right) Sam Bartram Collection; Page 40 Bartram family collection; Page 41 Bartram family collection; Page 43 Bartram family collection; Page 44 Bartram family collection; Page 45 Bartram family collection; Page 48 Sam Bartram Collection; Page 49 Bartram family collection; Page 51 Bartram family collection; Page 55 (bottom) Bartram family collection; Page 59 British Pathé; Page 61 British Pathé; Page 65 Empics; Page 66 Empics; Page 68 Syndication International; Page 69 British Pathé; Page 70 Empics; Page 74 British Pathé; Page 75 Getty Images; Page 77 Sam Bartram Collection; Page 79 Bartram family collection; Page 80 Sam Bartram Collection; Page 83 (top) Sam Bartram Collection; Page 85 Sam Bartram Collection; Page 86 Sam Bartram Collection; Page 89 Sam Bartram Collection; Page 90 Sam Bartram Collection; Page 91 Empics; Page 93 (top and bottom left) Sam Bartram Collection (bottom right) Bartram family collection; Page 95 Sam Bartram Collection; Page 96 London FA; Page 97 (top) London FA (bottom) Bartram family collection; Page 101 Sam Bartram Collection; Page 103 Bartram family collection; Page 104 British Library Newspapers; Page 105 Sam Bartram Collection; Page 108 Sam Bartram Collection; Page 109 Sam Bartram Collection; Page 111 Sam Bartram Collection; Page 114 Sam Bartram Collection; Page 116 (top) Sam Bartram Collection (bottom) Derek Lloyd; Page 117 Sam Bartram Collection; Page 118 (top left and right) Sam Bartram Collection (bottom) Playfair Football Annual; Page 119 (bottom) Empics; Page 122 Empics; Page 123 Sam Bartram Collection; Page 125 Sam Bartram Collection; Page 126 Sam Bartram Collection; Page 130 Tempus Publishing; Page 131 (bottom) Popperfoto; Page 132 (top) David Batters (bottom left) Sam Bartram Collection (bottom right) Bartram family collection; Page 133 Empics; Page 136 Sam Bartram collection; Page 137 Sam Bartram Collection; Page 138 Bartram family collection; Page 139 Bartram family collection; Page 140 Bartram family collection; Page 151 Sam Bartram Collection; Page 152 (right) Bartram family collection; Page 155 Charlton Athletic FC; Page 170 *Gazette* Blackpool; Page 177 Bartram family collection; Page 178 Sam Bartram Collection; Page 180 Sam Bartram Collection; all other images from author's archives.

PREFACE

'I made up my mind that I was going to tell the crowd how wonderful they and everyone else connected with Charlton had been to me; how much I had loved and enjoyed every minute of my time at The Valley and that no footballer had ever been so kindly treated. But when I got into the directors box and looked into that sea of friendly faces, and found the microphone in my hand, I was lost.

No matter how I tried, all I could do was to stammer out "Thank you, thank you so much" and leave it at that. But I believe everyone understood just how I felt.'

Sam Bartram addressing the crowd after his last game for Charlton. From Sam Bartram by Himself, *published in 1956.*

'Watching him pack his bags for an away game, his old goalkeeping sweater with holes in it, his beaten-up boots, watching him mend his goalkeeping gloves and old cap, his misshapen hands from years of playing in goal, listening to a complete replay of the game – pass by pass, kick by kick – after he came home from the match are some of the goalkeeping memories of my father.

I don't remember much about his last game except for my father's emotion when he said goodbye to the fans. I had never seen him overcome by emotion like that before. He was genuinely sad to be leaving Charlton and the club's loyal fans.'

Sam's daughter, Moira, on the occasion of Charlton's centenary match, October 2004.

INTRODUCTION

Not so very long ago, if your name was Bartram, chances are your schoolmates, work colleagues or service pals would have nicknamed you 'Sam'. Such was the fame and popularity of Charlton Athletic's outstanding goalkeeper of the 1930s, 1940s and 1950s.

In Sam Bartram's day goalkeepers were an unprotected species, at the mercy of marauding forwards wearing hard toe-capped boots and a football that approached the weight of a medicine ball in the often wet and muddy conditions. Despite these hazards Sam was fearless and indestructible, missing only a handful of Football League games in almost twenty-two years at The Valley.

Charlton manager Jimmy Seed signed Bartram on trial from Tyneside club Boldon Villa in 1934. He was granted an extended run in the reserve team before becoming a full-time professional two months later. After a short while he established himself as Charlton's number one. Once Sam became a senior-team regular, he was never dropped and remained first choice until he retired at the age of forty-two in 1956!

All of Charlton's greatest moments have come with Bartram in the team, Jimmy Seed at the helm and, more often than not, Don Welsh as captain. The rise from the Third Division to runners-up in the top division in consecutive seasons in the late 1930s was a feat that has not been equalled since and was followed by successive FA Cup finals as runners-up then winners in the immediate postwar years. Bartram himself played in four consecutive Wembley finals between 1944 and 1947 and was only denied five in a row because service commitments kept him out of the 1943 wartime showpiece.

The majority of his remarkable tally of 800 appearances were made in the old First Division, making Sam a favourite not just in south-east London but on other grounds around the country. His flamboyant style and personality endeared him to the widest audience in the days before regular television coverage and super-stardom were part of the game. Bartram was to Charlton as Matthews was to Stoke, Finney to Preston and Milburn to Newcastle – a local hero who was greatly respected throughout the land.

His green roll-neck sweater, ample shorts, red-and-white socks and ankle-high boots now cut an antique look but here was a super-fit athlete whose physique is reputed to have inspired artist Picasso and frequently defied the top goal scorers of his time. Goalkeepers wore no names or numbers on their jerseys in those days and in Charlton's case there was no need, for Sam, with his distinctive wavy 'red' hair, was known everywhere.

For generations, Bartram in goal for Charlton was a national institution, like *Two-Way Family Favourites* and *The Billy Cotton Band Show*. His name was synonymous with the club. When Sam set a Football League record of 500 games for one club in 1954, Charlton changed the name of the turnstiles at the Lansdowne Mews corner of the ground from the Laundry End to the Sam Bartram Entrance, surely an unprecedented honour for a current footballer. It did not stop there, for, after Charlton took the field to the tune of *The Red, Red, Robin,* as they still do, the music would change to *Sam's Song,* the signature tune of comedian Sam Costa.

During Bartram's long spell in the Charlton goal, Britain was ruled by four separate monarchs and crowds at The Valley reached their peak, with attendances of over 70,000 recorded on several occasions. In those pre-television days the relationship between players and supporters was a more personal one. Nevertheless, famous footballers were often accorded superhuman status and Sam's heroics saw him likened to fictional characters Dan Dare, Superman and the Pied Piper!

In truth, he was more a 'Roy of the Rovers'. At fourteen, young Bartram was selected at wing half for England schoolboys – at a time when football featured on the curriculum of most schools in the land. While still in his teens, he was a free-scoring centre forward in northern non-league football. At twenty he joined Charlton as a goalkeeper. Seventy-one years later, when the club celebrated its centenary, their supporters – many of whom had never seen him play – were so inspired by his legacy that they voted Sam the club's greatest ever 'keeper. What's more, all Charlton's special centenary awards were in the form of a Bartram statuette and dubbed the 'Sammys'.

one

GROWING UP IN COUNTY DURHAM

Sam was born at Simonside, an area of South Shields close to the south bank of the River Tyne, just before the First World War. South Shields was a thriving port shipping locally mined coal and importing timber from Northern Europe. Ships often filled the river as they waited for a berth at Tyne Dock, just upstream from Shields. Indicative of the size and importance of the river trade, plus mining and shipbuilding, was the fact that more than 120 butchers' shops supported the town and its busy industries.

Despite being one of the heaviest industrial areas in the world at that time, County Durham boasted many recreational outlets, with brass bands and football leading the way, amid beautiful countryside and miles of sandy beaches. However, these were Spartan times and the attractions of the latter were often restricted to high days and holidays. For much of the year the miners seldom saw daylight, clocking on before sunrise and leaving work in the dusk. It was arduous and dangerous work, often in cramped, damp conditions deep underground.

The Bartram family moved a few miles south to Boldon Colliery, a purpose-built mining village, before Sam, the youngest of three boys, reached school age. It was here that he learned his football. Encouraged by his father, also named Sam, a miner and former winger with King's Park in Scotland, he developed a love for the game that was to dominate his life. Sam Bartram senior fought with distinction in the famous Durham Light Infantry during the First World War and, like so many unfortunate soldiers, suffered the terrible effects of gas in the trenches on the European front, never fully recovering. Young Sam was just nine years of age when his father died.

By now he was playing impromptu games of football whenever and wherever possible. Sam's early games were like those of many aspiring professionals, played with a tin can in the street, or with a makeshift ball of newspaper. To kick a real ball, even a small rubber one, was an occasional luxury that only came about if given one by neighbours in return for running errands.

Boldon Colliery Miners Lodge with brass band and banners *c.* 1925.

Boldon Colliery Homing Pigeon Club with cup *c.* 1920.

Boldon Villa FC *c.* 1920.

Fortunately a new master at Boldon Colliery School, George Gair, set about raising a football team and this proved to be Sam's big chance. His enthusiasm blossomed. When kicking around with schoolmates he always favoured being in goal but captained the school team from half-back. After representing the school on Saturday mornings Sam and his friends would travel on foot to watch either Sunderland or Newcastle play in the afternoon, sometimes running part of the way to ensure a good spot at the front of the crowd. There was no money for bus fares in those days and Boldon was six miles from Newcastle and four from Sunderland. Nevertheless, it was from the terraces at Roker Park, Sunderland, and St James' Park, Newcastle, that he eagerly watched the leading players of the 1920s, who fuelled his ambition to become a professional footballer himself and to one day play in a Wembley cup final.

Inspired by his heroes, scheming inside forward Hughie Gallacher of Newcastle and wing half and penalty king Bill Clunas of Sunderland, the young Bartram learned fast. His school team won the local league and cup and he was selected for Sunderland District Schoolboys where, in the 1927/28 season, he played alongside Raich Carter from Hendon School, who was later to become one of Sunderland's all-time great footballers. The team won 4 out of 4 matches, beating Lambton & Hetton 4-0, Tynemouth 6-2, Chester-le-Street 5-0 and Derwent Valley 6-1 and reached the semi-final of the English Schools' Shield, but lost 1-2 to Preston Schools, despite skipper Carter bursting the Preston net from the penalty spot. The 1927/28 Sunderland Schools line-up was: Purdy (Barnes); Dryer (James William Street), Forrest (Hudson Road); Hannah (Hudson Road), Farrow (Whitburn), Bartram (Boldon Colliery); Laing (St Columba's), Lumsdon (Castleton), Taylor (New Silksworth), Carter (Hendon), Elliott (Colliery).

Above left: Boldon Colliery Leek Club members with leeks *c.* 1920.

Above right: Hughie Gallacher, who led Newcastle to the Football League Championship in 1927.

That year Sam also captained County Durham Schools, for which he was awarded a cap, and scored the goal in a 1-0 win over neighbours Northumberland. His performance earned him a call-up for England Schoolboys but he was denied the chance of an international cap because in the meantime, to help support his family in difficult times, he had started work at Boldon Colliery. Fourteen-year-old Bartram, the boy miner, heard of his selection a few days later. This must have been a bitter disappointment not only for Sam but especially for his mother, who gave him every encouragement by watching most of his matches. She even allowed him to stay on at school for a while after reaching the leaving age of fourteen, just in case the England honour for which he was being tipped came his way.

The England Schoolboys team that beat Scotland 5-0 in April 1928, without Bartram, was: W.H. Roper (Conway Street School, Birkenhead); R.W. Stuart (Marton Grove School, Middlesbrough), R.F. Trim (Winton & Moordown School, Bournemouth, Captain); G.W. Taylor (Ellis Avenue School, Leicester), W. Ives (Stoke School, Guildford), W.F. Puffett (Gorse Hill School, Swindon); A. Geldart (Whetley Lane School, Bradford), J.F. McGovern (Eglinton Road School, Woolwich), W.J. Howlett (Wilson Senior School, Reading), H.S. Carter (Hendon School, Sunderland), R. Stockill (Poppleton Road School, York).

In the 1920s County Durham boasted five Football League clubs, Sunderland, Darlington, Durham City, Hartlepools United and South Shields. The major non-league competitions were the North-East League, Northern League and Wearside League. Throughout the region there was a spread of semi-professional and amateur soccer that linked town, village, company and colliery clubs. These included a host of famous names like Bishop Auckland, Crook Town, Tow Law, Evenwood Town, Billingham Synthonia, Willington, Ferryhill Athletic, Shildon, Spennymoor United, Stockton and West Auckland Town. All of these clubs and indeed others, in competitions like the South Tyne Alliance, took the game very seriously and attracted considerable support. It was the perfect environment for the development of a young aspiring professional player.

After leaving Boldon Colliery School, Sam followed his brothers into the mining industry. There was precious little alternative for school leavers looking to earn their first wage packet then, other than perhaps a highly sought-after job at the local co-op store. In 1928, when he first went underground, the mines were just recovering from the General Strike and lockout of 1926 and this meant one of his elder brothers had been laid off, so Sam's contribution, as a family breadwinner for his mother, brothers and three sisters, was vital. As a fourteen-year-old his wage was low but without it things would have been impossible for the Bartram family.

When coal production was in full swing at Boldon Colliery in the 1930s, 2,000 miners were employed. The workforce was renowned locally for its closeness and there was a strong sense of community. They were employed by

Top left: Boldon Colliery pithead.

Top right: 1930s Boldon miner's lamp.

Above: A group of Boldon miners pictured in the late 1920s.

Left: A Miner's coin issued by Boldon Industrial Co-operative Society.

the Harton Coal Company, who also operated nearby Whitburn and Harton Collieries. Boldon had the luxury of the first pithead baths in County Durham, opened in February 1927 and, on the initiative of the miners, the first Aged Miners' Homes in the Durham coalfield had been built in Hedworth Lane, Boldon Colliery, in 1914.

Mining was a hazardous occupation and although the three pits at Boldon escaped any major disasters, there were fatalities. Fortunately for the Bartram family, they saw the funny side when Sam's brother Benny was briefly trapped underground on account of his extra large feet, but such an incident only illustrated the ever-present dangers of working in such a restricted environment.

There was a saying in the North-East, 'If you're looking for a centre forward, just whistle down the nearest mineshaft.' In Sam's case they must have changed the tune from time to time, for he would follow a shift underground by turning out for local clubs at half-back, centre forward or goalkeeper! At first he continued in his schoolboy position of left half for the village team Boldon Villa. His performances in senior football proved good enough to get him noticed by scouts from other clubs and the news that a Football League club was showing interest kept him on top form. Tynesiders Jarrow persuaded Sam to sign for them, using the bait of a better chance of league football but, after just 2 games, he returned to Boldon. Almost immediately he was offered a trial by Reading of the Football League and it was an excited seventeen-year-old who made the long journey south for the first time.

Sam played in 4 matches for Reading reserves in the London Combination League at right half. He found the standard far superior to that to which he was accustomed in the North-East and at the end of a month's trial it was back to Boldon Villa. Reading manager Joe Smith helped Sam with personal coaching and encouragement but unfortunately he did not make the grade and headed home disappointed, but more determined than ever to eventually succeed as a professional. This determination saw him convinced that left half should be his regular position on the field and later, when Boldon Villa selected him at centre forward against his wishes, he took off and tried his luck with North Shields in the North-East League and Easington Colliery in the Wearside League.

It seems the committee at Boldon were not alone in thinking that a super-fit six-footer would make a natural centre forward, because both Easington and North Shields played Sam up front to good effect. On his debut for Easington he scored a hat-trick in the local derby with Murton Colliery and Alceste, reporting on North Shields in the *Football Gazette* of September 1933, reports, 'Speaking of dash reminds me of Sammy Bartram, a relation of the ex-Shields (now Falkirk) leader, who is playing centre forward for the reserves. Sammy is very reminiscent of his namesake's methods – no finesse but plenty of energy and pluck. On Wednesday he performed a hat-trick against Newcastle West End, when he was always on the spot when needed. His first goal, headed from a fine cross by Shepherd, was a perfect gem of timing. With some ball control, Bartram will take some stopping. The backs he plays against find he needs some stopping even without it!'

This was evidently the case shortly afterwards, when he lined-up for Shields first team in a midweek home game against Howdon at Appleby Park, North

Shields, when Sam was among the goal scorers in a 6-0 victory. The following Saturday he failed to find the net as the Robins went down 1-5 to Middlesbrough reserves at Ayresome Park. This spell at North Shields was rewarding in many ways, not least because the 'three half-crowns' expenses for each match (less than 50p in today's currency) was a useful addition to his low wage from the coalface, but also an important lesson was learnt from trainer Alan Grenier, the former South Shields and Everton left half. This experienced ex-pro impressed on Sam the benefit of playing in different positions, thus gaining an overall perspective on team play. From this time on he became more objective in his philosophy of the game and ceased to complain about playing in the forward line.

What became more of an issue was the travelling involved in playing at this top level of non-league football, plus the disappointment that, despite his goal scoring feats attracting the attention of scouts from professional clubs, no offers were forthcoming. So once again Sam felt he had not made the grade. He recalls, 'travelling to North Shields was getting quite a rush journey for me, especially as I had to work in the mine on Saturdays. I used to start at 4 a.m. and finish at 12 noon. So I just had time to rush home, have a bath and a snack before an hour's journey on the bus. So realising my football was being affected, I finished there and returned once again to Boldon Villa.'

This was early in the 1933/34 season and Sam re-established himself at left half in the village team. A local report of the match between Corinthians and Boldon Villa at White's Field, South Shields, in December 1933 reads, 'Bartram scored a picture goal, beating man after man, from his own half of the field and finally having Goodall well-beaten with a powerful shot from twenty yards range.' Three months later, after Boldon beat South Shields Adelaide 5-1 in the second replay of a cup semi-final, his big break came and it could not have been more unexpected. Suddenly, all those long years of aspirations as a would-be goalkeeper – as a schoolboy in made-up games, at Boldon Villa training sessions and even during his month's trial at Reading, where he annoyed manager Joe Smith by habitually taking up a position in goal during shooting practice – were to pay off.

The *Football Gazette* of Saturday 24 March announced under 'South Tyne Alliance Topics', 'Pymans and Boldon Villa to meet at Stanley Street. Once again the time has arrived for the deciding of our league challenge cup final and, for the information of those who may be interested, the game will take place on Good Friday, commencing at 3.15, at Middle Dock's ground, Stanley Street, Tyne Dock. The contesting teams on this occasion are Pymans (Tyne Dock), the present holders, and Boldon Villa, the present league champions. In these two clubs we have material enough to provide an attractive final.'

A subsequent *Gazette* report read, 'The Tyne Alliance Challenge Cup Final was played off on Good Friday at Stanley Street between Pyman's and Boldon Villa. Orders were issued by the police, I understand, to close the gate as there was a possibility of the crowd getting out of hand if further increased but everything

went off quite smoothly, although it must be said that only a very much interrupted view of the game was obtained by those who arrived at the last minute
and evidently did not expect to see such a crowd. The score is recorded as a 0-0
draw, with a replay scheduled for Saturday 21 April, at Harton Colliery Athletic
enclosure, Green Lane.' According to the reporter, 'Referee Ord of Washington
had a good game and was right to disallow a goal for Boldon.' He had, 'an
uninterrupted view of the whole situation and had no hesitation in deciding
no goal.'

What, perhaps rather surprisingly, is not mentioned is that Boldon Villa might
have had a goalkeeping crisis. Regular custodian Alec Knowles was injured but
aspiring 'keeper Sam Bartram persuaded the club to let him switch from left half
to keep goal and he played a major part in the goal-less draw.

By the time the replay came round, Knowles was fit again and resumed in
goal, with Sam back in the left half berth. The Villa won 2-1 after extra time,
there being no score after ninety minutes, and took the cup on the short journey
back to Boldon Colliery. However, it was the original game, on Friday 30 March,
that was to launch the long and distinguished career of Bartram the goalkeeper.
Unknown to Sam, in the crowd at Tyne Dock that afternoon was Anthony Seed
from Whitburn, a colliery village close to Boldon. He was an elder brother of

From the *Football Gazette*, 7 April 1934.

From the *Football Gazette*, 28 April 1934.

Jimmy Seed, the former Sunderland inside forward and England international, who was then in his first season as manager of London club Charlton Athletic. Seed senior regularly advised his brother of promising talent in the area and that day Boldon Villa goalkeeper Bartram's performance caught his eye and he was added to the list.

A few weeks later Sam was back in goal for Boldon, when a report of their league title-chasing game with South Shields Adelaide reads, 'Victory to Adelaide last Saturday would have given them the honours for the second successive season. Boldon were successful by 4-3 and they owe much to custodian 'Sammy' Bartram and 'Billy' Tate, the outside right, who scored all four goals for his side.'

Sam was still Boldon Villa's goalkeeper at the start of the 1934/35 campaign as they beat Waldon Villa 5-1, with the *Football Gazette* stating, 'S. Bartram, the Boldon custodian, made many excellent saves during the game, while Smith at centre half was an outstanding player.' By now Bartram had been a coal miner on and off for over six years but there was no guarantee of continued employment. Then, in late summer 1934, when he was out of work, a tragedy struck Charlton Athletic. Their goalkeeper Alec Wright had been outstanding in a midweek win at Torquay United but, in the time off that the team had been granted afterwards, he was fatally injured in a bathing accident.

Manager Jimmy Seed swiftly followed up the recommendation of his brother some month's earlier and Anthony Seed was sent to offer the makeshift Boldon goalkeeper a month's trial at Charlton. For Sam this was third time lucky. Having failed to become a professional footballer as wing half or centre forward, here was the opportunity to make the grade in his favourite position of goalkeeper. Events moved fast. A rushed meeting took place with Anthony Seed on a street corner near the Bartram's Boldon home. Sam recalls, 'The introductions were soon over and there, before some rather curious passers-by, I signed for a month's trial at The Valley.'

His miner's wage was 17s 6d per week (less than 88p today) and, at the time of joining Charlton in September 1934, he was drawing 14s 3d unemployment benefit (approx 72p), with a sixpenny subscription (2.5p) to the football team towards referees' fees. Being offered £5 a week by Charlton made him feel like a millionaire. Sam didn't tell his mother of the Charlton offer until he was packing for the journey. As ever, she gave him every support, as he set off determined to succeed this time around.

There was a friendly reunion when Sam stepped down from the train at London's King's Cross station. Manager Seed had thoughtfully sent Matt Forster, also a native of the North-East, to meet the new arrival. The pair had previously met when Sam was on trial at Reading. They set off together for digs in Charlton.

A couple of days later, on Saturday 15 September, instead of turning out for Boldon Villa, twenty-year-old Bartram made his Charlton debut in the reserves at Kenilworth Road, Luton. What a baptism of fire that turned out to be – Charlton lost 0-6. Fortunately for a disappointed Sam, Alex Hird, the team trainer, said he was not to blame for any of the goals and that he gave a 'promising' display. Then a 2-4 reverse against West Ham reserves was followed by defeat at the hands of Tottenham Hotspur, but at least the trial period ended with a 2-1 win over Portsmouth.

Manager Seed called the disconsolate young goalkeeper to his office to review his first month and granted a further four weeks' trial, with the advice that he had to do much better in order to make the grade. A determined Bartram practiced all the hours he could and, with the encouragement of fellow Geordie – trainer Jimmy Trotter – and his teammates, his improvement was noticeable. This was put to the test in the final match of his two-month stint in a midweek reserve team game with Chelsea at Stamford Bridge. Sam was on his toes, eager to succeed right from the first minute of the match, encouraged by a promise from Jimmy Seed that a good display would see him signed on permanently.

He was helped in his cause by Chelsea gaining plenty of scoring opportunities and Sam twice collided with a post in saving 'certain' goals. An elated Bartram left the field confident he had played a major part in the 2-1 victory. On reaching the dressing room he found Jimmy Seed already there and, after congratulating his aspiring 'keeper, the manager offered what Sam had craved for so long, a full-time professional contract with a Football League club. An ambition was fulfilled. His total delight is recorded in his autobiography; 'The sober and respectable residents of Charlton must have been astonished, that late afternoon, to see a red-headed youth almost dancing with joy as he hurriedly made his way to his digs in Maryon Road.'

The joy and pleasure felt by Sam Bartram that mid-November day was never to be extinguished throughout a lifetime in football. There must have been times when he felt he was on the brink of having to catch the train home. Thoughts of his family and friends back in the North-East, all wishing him well, drove him on, determined to succeed in what he felt to be his last chance to become a professional player. Jimmy Seed's role was crucial too. There is no doubting he was a managerial genius, as later years proved. He liked what he saw in the character of the young Bartram and backed brother Anthony's judgment of his goalkeeping ability to the hilt. The manager took an instant liking to Sam and must have been willing him to make the grade. It was the beginning of a wonderful friendship and the most exciting time in Charlton's history. Sam could not wait to send a letter home to announce the good news.

Charlton had started the 1934/35 Third Division (South) campaign in promising fashion, winning 8 and drawing 3 of the first 15 games. In the 1-1 draw at Northampton on 17 November they were forced to play for eighty minutes with ten men. Forward George Robinson took over in goal when 'keeper Harry Wright was taken to hospital following a ninth-minute injury. The following Saturday Cliff Owen was the Addicks' goalkeeper during the drawn home first round FA Cup tie with Exeter City and also played in the 2-5 defeat in the replay at Exeter a few days later.

So it was a surprised Bartram who received his big chance much sooner than anticipated. Jimmy Seed called him up for the next Third Division match and encouraged a nervous Sam to play his normal game. The manager put him at ease, advising that he had every confidence in him and added the team would also give every encouragement. With these assurances Charlton's new goalkeeper ran out for his first Football League match at Vicarage Road, Watford, on Saturday 1 December. He kept a clean sheet in the first half but was twice beaten by opposing centre forward Carter later on, as the home side finished 2-0 winners. The full Charlton line-up was: Sam Bartram; Norman Smith, Jimmy Oakes; Joe Jobling, Frank Harris, Bill Dodgin; Monty Wilkinson, George Robinson, Ralph Allen, George Stephenson, Harold Hobbis. Jimmy Seed's diary entry for the match read, 'Bartram; Played very well. Safe, confident.'

The manager selected the same eleven for the next game and was rewarded with a 6-0 home win over Newport County. Thus The Valley faithful, 10,186 on this occasion, were introduced to their future favourite son. Although, in fact,

Charlton Athletic Third Division (South) champions 1934/35: From left to right, back row: Frank Rist, Joe Jobling, George Robinson, Sam Bartram, Norman Smith, Bert Turner, Jimmy Trotter (Trainer). Front row: Monty Wilkinson, George Stephenson, Ralph Allen, Jimmy Seed (Secretary/Manager), Les Boulter, Harold Hobbis, Don Welsh.

Harry Wright was back in goal a week later and remained there for a run of 5 matches during which Charlton were unbeaten, Wright fell victim to injury again at the end of December. So 1935 started with Bartram back in goal and he kept his place for a run of 16 matches, twelve of which were won, including 'derby' games with Millwall, Crystal Palace, Queens Park Rangers and Clapton Orient. Harry Wright returned for the last 4 matches, by which time promotion was almost assured.

Strengthened by the signing of wing half Don Welsh from Torquay United and centre forward Ralph Allen from Brentford, Charlton finished the 1934/35 season as clear champions. A Third Division winners' medal in his first season was an auspicious start to Sam's professional career, but not even the most optimistic players or fans could have imagined what was to follow. Promotion to the Second Division brought a new challenge for a Charlton team that had blended well during the previous season.

There was also a particular attraction for the club's large northern contingent – 2 matches with Newcastle United. The new term started with Harry Wright in goal, and a 4-0 home victory over Burnley was followed by a 0-3 defeat away to Manchester United. Match three, away to Doncaster Rovers, saw Sam make his Second Division bow and he was called upon for all but one league game during the remainder of 1935/36 season. A particular Bartram highlight was the 2-1 win

Above: Sam in action during a practice match at The Valley, 1935. Also in the picture are Ralph Allen, Frank Rist and Bert Tann.

Right: An early press portrait.

over Newcastle at St James' Park, with Charlton taking an early two-goal lead through Welsh and Allen.

This was a special occasion for Sam, returning to the ground where he regularly watched from the terraces on Saturday afternoons as a spellbound schoolboy. His mother Mary was in the crowd, as she had been at Boldon and many other places during Sam's earlier football career. Family and friends were regular supporters whenever he returned north with Charlton and this was the first time as a professional. Proud Sam could hardly wait to run out onto that familiar old ground. When Charlton went 2-0 ahead in just six minutes, life couldn't get much better. The only blow was, during the half-time interval, he discovered a gash in his right calf that required seven stitches courtesy of the Newcastle medical officer. Fortunately it didn't impair his performance and almost as importantly did not require him to return to London for treatment straight away. So it was back to North Road Boldon Colliery for the weekend with his mother, sisters and brothers. What a reunion that must have been.

A few months later Charlton completed the double over Newcastle with a 4-2 Wednesday afternoon victory and Bartram hit the headlines. One national newspaper proclaimed, 'Bartram the Wonder Man Pulls Charlton Through' and added, 'You have to hand it to red-headed Sam Bartram, Charlton goalkeeper. Many of his saves would make classic Harry Hibbs shudder. Yet he gets there. He

A save during a cup tie with Clapton Orient at Lea Bridge Road in January 1936. This was Sam's FA Cup debut, the first of 44 consecutive appearances in the competition.

Charlton Athletic Second Division runners–up 1935/36. From left to right, back row: Joe Jobbing, Bert Turner, Sam Bartram, Jimmy Oakes, Don Welsh, John Oakes. Front row: Monty Wilkinson, George Robinson, Stan Prior, George Stephenson, Harold Hobbis.

invents saves – and there is no doubt he was the turning point in yesterday's game against Newcastle United at The Valley. Yes, Bartram is a 'keeper with a style of his own. You expect mistakes but get thrills instead.' Another headline read, 'Redhead With A Style All His Own, Foiled Newcastle.'

Sam's fast-growing reputation in the game prompted him to be invited to test a prototype protective helmet that had been designed as a result of a number of serious injuries to players around that time. W.R.G. Smith, sports editor of the *Sunday Express*, in a feature on 1 March 1936, wrote, 'GOALKEEPERS TEST NEW CRASH HELMET. LIKE A SCULL CAP WITH MOVEABLE PEAK. Forget all the troubles in sport for a moment and let me tell you of football's latest introduction to preserve the craniums of goalkeepers. The suggestion that goalkeepers should wear crash helmets was first made by a reader in these columns. The idea has borne fruit. A leading firm of sports outfitters is going ahead with arrangements to put the helmet on the market. Certain modifications will have to be made but at the moment it resembles an ordinary motor-cycling helmet on a small scale. Made of leather, with an asbestos lining, the weight will be less than eight ounces. It will have a detachable flexible peak and the back will be close fitting like a scull cap, only coming lower on the neck. Straps will fasten under the chin. Sam Bartram, of Charlton, the most daring and unorthodox goalkeeper in the south, tried the new helmet for our benefit. "It would help goalkeepers a lot if adopted," said Sam. "No more bumps and bruises to doctor on Saturday nights! It would give us confidence, too, in diving for the ball at the feet of forwards. You can't protect all the body. The head is the main thing. That is where we get hurt

Charlton Athletic Football Club.

Record Achievement—3rd. Division (*Southern Section*) Champions 1934–35. Promotion to 1st. Division 1935–36.

BACK ROW: A. Hird. Boulter. Rist. J. Oakes. Bartram. Welsh. Turner. Stephenson. J. Trotter. (*Trainer*)

SEATED: Wilkinson. Oakes. (*Capt.*) J. M. Seed. Esq. (*Sec. Manager*) Prior. Hobbis.

FRONT ROW: Smith. Jobling. Robinson.

Charlton's record breakers.

most." Charlton's manager, Mr Jimmy Seed, also gave the helmet his approval. "Most clubs don't keep more than two or three goalkeepers on the books," he said. "When one is injured it causes a deal of inconvenience and perhaps the loss of valuable points. Goalkeepers often get their heads cut and bruised. A crash helmet would reduce the minor casualties.'"

The proposed helmet was, however, not a success and did not go into mass production.

By now a second successive promotion was looking a distinct possibility. Charlton had topped the Second Division for the first time a few weeks before and were unbeaten since. A great run saw only one defeat between early February and the end of the season, when Port Vale visited The Valley with the Addicks needing one point for a place in the First Division. A match report headline read, 'BARTRAM DEFIANT, NATURE, MAN, AND HURT COULD NOT BEAT HIM'. The report went on, 'Bartram is a giant in build and a giant in courage. He threw himself once at the feet of Roberts and got himself hurt. But he saved a certain goal. A minute later he saved another and got himself hurt again. He was magnificent. But for Bartram I think Port Vale would have stolen the match in the second half.'

Fortunately they didn't and the 1-1 scoreline not only saw Charlton through an unbeaten season at The Valley for the first time but also into the runners-up spot, one point behind Second Division champions Manchester United. This second successive promotion, which set a new Football League record, was achieved with a style based on a sound defence marshalled by captain Jimmy Oakes. The critics said it wouldn't last but they were proved wrong and were forced to eat their words for some time yet. For the twenty-two-year-old Bartram things were looking good and getting even better. In less than two years since travelling south for a trial, he was to become a regular in the First Division.

two

LIFE AT THE TOP

Prior to Charlton competing in the First Division for the first time in 1936/37, Jimmy Seed called the players together to give them the benefit of his knowledge of playing at the top level. This tutorage was to prove yet another managerial masterstroke as his team entered what was for them uncharted territory. The Charlton manager had a vast experience gained from his days as a player with Sunderland, Tottenham Hotspur, Sheffield Wednesday and England. The young Bartram listened intently to someone he admired and with whom he was to develop a lasting friendship. They were soul mates, having grown up in the same part of the North-East and both started work in the mines, Bartram at Boldon and Seed at Whitburn, adjacent collieries, both owned by the Harton Coal Company.

Sam credits these friendly discussions between manager and players with developing the outstanding spirit and teamwork that prevailed at the club, which was a significant factor in Charlton's rise to the top and in keeping them there for so long.

Jimmy Seed had packed away his working clothes on being signed by Sunderland in 1914, the year Bartram was born. He served in the First World War, joined Mid Rhondda in 1919 and moved to London a year later. He won an FA Cup winners' medal with Spurs in 1921, before helping Sheffield Wednesday to the Football League championship in 1929 and again in 1930. Two years as secretary-manager at Clapton Orient had prepared him for a similar role at Charlton. He had been persuaded to move across the Thames by the Addicks in 1933.

When the long-awaited First Division season of 1936/37 finally arrived Charlton found themselves on the road, with opening fixtures at Grimsby Town and Stoke City. They were rewarded with a win and a draw within three days. Then a 1-1 result at home to Liverpool, on the second Saturday of the season in front of 31,301, was followed by a visit from Stoke City, complete with Stanley Matthews, just two days later. Two second-half goals brought a 2-0 victory and the Addicks had opened their First Division era with six points out of eight. Not bad for a club that had only entered the Football League fifteen years earlier.

Above: Bert Turner watches as Sam foils a West Bromwich Albion attack in October 1936.

Left: Jimmy Seed in his playing days.

Opposite: Sam assisted by centre half John Oakes (centre) during a goalmouth tussle with Arsenal in the 1930s.

After a short while in the top flight, Sam Bartram was again in the spotlight. Some sources tipped him as a future England goalkeeper. To quote one newspaper, 'There is a new challenger to Woodley coming along rapidly in Bartram of Charlton. Bartram takes crazy risks, they say, but so have all the great goalkeepers, back to the "craziest" of them all, Dicky Roose, whom I once saw on the halfway line in an England *v.* Wales match!' A less supportive scribe condemned him as, 'a danger to football.'

By now Bartram was unquestionably Charlton's number one 'keeper and during three memorable seasons prior to the Second World War, spring-heeled Sam enjoyed football's life at the top, playing in all but one of the club's league and cup matches during that period. He relished pitting himself against the best in the game and although every match had its highlights, the home game with Birmingham City in mid-September was special, for it was the first time Sam had been on the field along with the great England goalkeeper Harry Hibbs.

Hibbs was a master of positional play and had a very attentive student that afternoon, watching his every move like a hawk, from the other end of the pitch. He was Bartram's idol, his ideal goalkeeper. Sam observed that Hibbs was always calm, nothing seemed to upset him, and he made goalkeeping look easy. Fortunately for Charlton he was beaten twice when centre forward Stan Prior and wing half Joe Jobling wiped out Birmingham's 2-0 half-time lead with two goals in four minutes early in the second-half.

Running out at the famous Highbury Stadium for the first time was another of Sam's great thrills. Matches between Charlton and Arsenal were considered local affairs by many in south-east London. Arsenal were founded at nearby Woolwich Arsenal and originally played on Plumstead Common. The Gunners had remained nearby until moving north to Highbury in 1913. Consequently there were more than 60,000 inside Highbury that afternoon and others were left stranded when the gates were closed before kick-off. A 1-1 draw saw Alf Kirchen score for Arsenal early in the second half, then the home team's Cliff Bastin shot wide from a penalty minutes later. Inside right George Robinson equalised for the Addicks just before full time.

Earlier in the season when Arsenal visited The Valley, it was their first match in the Woolwich area for twenty-three years. The attendance reflected this, with a Charlton ground record for a league match being set at 68,160, although it's thought that nearer 80,000 were in the ground. Arsenal became the first First Division club to win at The Valley, with goals from Davidson and Compton giving them a 2-0 victory. Both scores came when Charlton were below strength, with right-back Sid Cann off the field injured.

Above: Raich Carter (seated second left) and Sunderland's 1937 FA Cup-winning team.

Left: Spectators spill along the touchline as Sam saves against Arsenal.

It was the only home defeat of the season as newly promoted Charlton surprised the football world by challenging for the First Division championship. For Sam it must have seemed too good to be true, especially on 3 April 1937 when, three years since temporarily pulling on the Boldon Villa goalkeeper's jersey at nearby South Shields, he returned to his native County Durham as Charlton's established number one at Roker Park, Sunderland. What a day that must have been – reigning champions Sunderland were just one week away from an FA Cup semi-final and Charlton had their sights on league glory. The home skipper that day was Sam's colleague from the 1927/28 Sunderland Schools' team, Raich Carter, who a month later became the first captain of the Wearsiders to lift the FA Cup.

There was a significant contingent from Boldon Colliery in the ground, some with divided loyalties, as a proud Bartram ran out onto the familiar pitch and looked up to the spot behind the goal where he had stood so often as a schoolboy. There, waving and shouting a warm Roker welcome, were his boyhood friends. With the Bartram family also looking on, this was some special homecoming.

Although Sunderland won with the only goal of the game, a second-half strike from inside left Patrick Gallacher, Charlton were unbeaten in their subsequent fixtures and finished their first season in the top flight as runners-up to champions Manchester City. This was the second successive campaign that had seen them finish behind one of the Manchester clubs, as United had beaten them to the Second Division title just twelve months earlier. The season ended with a 2-1 home win over Brentford and Sam was headline news once again.

'SAM BARTRAM'S HARDEST TASK. "Mike" ordeal ends great season's work. Sam Bartram, Charlton goalkeeper, tackled the biggest task of his football

Charlton Athletic First Division runners-up 1936/37. From left to right, back row: John Oakes, Bert Turner, Sam Bartram, Don Welsh, Bert Tann. Front row: Monty Wilkinson, George Robinson, Jimmy Oakes, Les Boulter, Harold Hobbis, George Tadman.

career on Saturday. It was a task far harder than keeping shots out of his goal. An enthusiastic crowd gathered in front of the stand and would not go away until Bartram had made a speech to them. Bartram was changing, but wrapping a towel around himself he nervously went to the "mike". "Thanks so… thanks very… it's very nice of you," he stuttered. Bartram's play has had much to do with Charlton winning second position in the league and the unofficial championship of London. But the supporters had not only that to celebrate, for they had just seen Charlton make sure of their position with a well-earned victory in a great match.'

So, after less than three years as a full-time professional footballer, Sam had seen his club rise from the Third Division (South) to second place in the First Division. This was a remarkable achievement and Charlton shared with Arsenal the distinction of conceding the least number of First Division goals. Indeed, they were the most miserly team at home, with the visiting teams scoring only 13 times at The Valley.

In April they had also achieved another notable success, a 5-2 victory over the French national team. This was the first of Bartram's many visits abroad. The players, standing in at short notice for the Italian international team who had withdrawn from the fixture, left London by boat train following a 1-0 home win over Huddersfield Town on the Saturday and travelled overnight to Paris for the Sunday game. At half-time the scores were level at 2-2. Sam kept a clean sheet in the second period during which Charlton played 'copybook football' and scored three times, to record what must have been the club's most outstanding result in their thirty-two-year history.

These heady days of the late 1930s must have seen like one long adventure for the Charlton team, for in May 1937 they set sail on the RMS *Empress of Australia* bound for a six-week tour to Canada and the USA. Seventeen players were in the travelling party; Sam Bartram, Les Boulter, Sid Cann, George Green, Freddy Ford, Harold Hobbis, Joe Jobling, John Oakes, George Robinson, Jack Shreeve, George Stephenson, George Tadman, Bert Tann, Bert Turner, Don Welsh, Monty Wilkinson and Les Williams. Matches were played in New York, Pittsburgh, Detroit, Chicago, Calgary, Vancouver, Saskatchewan, Winnipeg, Toronto and Montreal. The tour opened in New York's all-seater Yankee Stadium – such outdoor facilities didn't exist at home at that time. There were also some other surprises for players used to English conditions, such as playing at night under floodlights in Pittsburgh, and several of the 13 matches took place on baked-hard grounds in searing heat – a totally new experience, especially for a goalkeeper from Tyneside!

Returning unbeaten from the USA and Canada, where the tourists recorded twelve wins and a draw, scoring 72 goals with just 9 against, must have been a

Charlton players and officials aboard the RMS *Empress of Australia* bound for Canada and the USA in May 1937.

useful prelude to Charlton's third season in the top flight back home. It was a sure confidence booster for everyone concerned and saw the 1937/38 season begin with Charlton unbeaten in the first 7 games, with just 5 goals against and top of the league.

Prior to the match at home to Middlesbrough, on the morning of Saturday 25 September, Sam married Charlton supporter Helen Richards at Our Lady of Grace Church, Charlton Road, Blackheath, opposite the famous Rectory Field, headquarters of Blackheath Rugby Club and a former Charlton Athletic home ground. Sam and Helen first met following a game soon after his arrival at Charlton. The wedding was national news. Jimmy Seed was there to make sure his valuable 'keeper was not delayed for the afternoon kick-off. Then, after a reception at Charlton Conservative Club, as he ran on to the pitch, just down the road, Sam was given a great welcome by the crowd and the Royal Artillery Band played excerpts from the wedding march. Ironically, Helen, who had not previously missed any of Sam's matches at The Valley, was left stranded at the reception while everyone else went off to the match.

The papers were full of reports and pictures. One local paper, describing the wedding, said, 'The wedding at Our Lady of Grace, Charlton Road, on Saturday morning, of Sam Bartram, Charlton Athletic's popular goalkeeper, to Miss Helen Richards of Charlton Lane, was quite a social event for the district. Scores of people were present both inside and outside the church and the happy couple

Sam and Helen on their wedding day. Jimmy Seed is on hand to make sure his 'keeper does not miss the afternoon kick-off.

Syd Jordan's impressions of the Charlton *v*. Middlesbrough match on Sam's wedding day.

were given a special cheer. Mr James Seed, the Charlton manager, was among the club representatives there and also members of both teams. The bride carried a bouquet of red and white flowers – the club colours – and after the ceremony there was a luncheon in the Charlton Conservative Club. Sam and his bride have taken up residence in Elliscombe Road, Charlton, which is only a short distance from The Valley ground. Mr Arthur Richards, a brother of the bride was the best man. Miss Alice Richards, a sister, was one of the bridesmaids. Miss Connie Meads was the other bridesmaid.'

The day ended well for Sam and Helen who were reunited after the game, which resulted in a 1-0 win for Charlton, keeping them at the top of the table, thanks to a Don Welsh goal and a fine Bartram display, which Sam later credited thus, 'I suppose it was the joy of being married that made me play so well.' A match report read, 'Sam Bartram, hero of the day – all bridegrooms are heroes on their wedding day – soon became a football hero, for in the fifth minute he made as grand a save as he ever will when parrying a really great shot by Fenton, launched with the speed of a rocket and true to its mark. Shot and save were truly magnificent.'

Next week, at the Victoria Ground, Stoke, Stanley Matthews proved Charlton's undoing as he set up two goals for the home side and ended the early season run. One national daily paper said, 'Bartram is the best goalkeeper I have seen for a long time. Charlton were completely second best. Only Bartram played really well and how grandly he played! This fellow knows his job alright, and he deserved the ovation which the crowd gave him as he went off.'

It can't have been too much of a surprise when the consistent Bartram was called-up for an England trial, prior to the first international of the season in Belfast. The teams selected were: Probables: Vic Woodley (Chelsea); Bert Sproston (Leeds United), Sam Barkas (Manchester City); Ken Willingham (Huddersfield Town), Alf Young (Huddersfield Town), Jackie Bray (Manchester City); Albert Geldard (Everton), Ray Bowden (Arsenal), Bob Gurney (Sunderland), Len Goulden (West Ham United), Eric Brook (Manchester City). Possibles: Sam Bartram (Charlton Athletic); Leslie Compton (Arsenal), Bob Stuart (Middlesbrough); Jack Crayston (Arsenal), Stan Cullis (Wolverhampton Wanderers), Wilf Copping (Arsenal); Alf Kirchen (Arsenal), Will Scott (Brentford), Billy Richardson (West Bromwich Albion), Eric Stephenson (Leeds United), Jimmy Morton (West Ham United).

Charlton manager Jimmy Seed and chairman Albert Gliksten travelled to Everton's Goodison Park to watch the Wednesday afternoon match, which finished in a 1-1 draw. A contemporary newspaper report concluded, 'Bartram played a great game for the Possibles at Liverpool, on Wednesday, but Woodley, the Chelsea goalkeeper, retains his place in the England team.' On the day that England played Northern Ireland in Belfast, Charlton met Bolton Wanderers at The Valley.

Alex James, the brilliant Scotland and Arsenal forward, writing about the game, said, 'The Charlton v. Bolton game at The Valley may not have supplied enough goals to satisfy the gluttons, but there was enough good football to satisfy me in conditions which became more difficult as time went on... Charlton had no go-ahead forward of the Westwood-type [Bolton inside-left], and it was only the brilliance of Bartram, who on two occasions saved point-blank from Westwood, and on another two occasions from Milsom, that enabled Charlton to escape their first home defeat of the season. I had heard a lot about Bartram and everything he did in this match bore out the good things my friends had told me. Not only did he accomplish all that is usually expected of a goalkeeper, but he showed intelligence in his fielding of the ball and in the confidence he obviously had in his backs and half-backs. He was not content merely to boot the ball up the field, but always tried to give to one of his own side, quite often by throwing or rolling it along the ground. I could understand why Charlton have had so few goals scored against them. They all believe in each other although at times they take chances.'

Three weeks later, following another 1-1 draw, this time with Wolves, Sam hit the headlines again. 'Great goalkeeping. Hats off to Bartram.' Brum, a midlands reporter wrote, 'With goalkeeper Bartram as the hero of a game which he repeatedly saved when all seemed lost, Charlton were very lucky to escape with

Sam at work on his boots.

Opposite and overleaf: Sporting Sam.

a point from Molyneux... Although their defenders had played splendidly in the first half, Charlton went to pieces in this department towards the end, and only the brilliance of Bartram intervened between them and defeat. The young north-country goalkeeper has rarely played a finer game since he came to Charlton.'

On Christmas Day 1937 Sam delivered another memorable performance. This time it was quite by accident. A crowd of over 40,000 were in holiday mood at Stamford Bridge, where Don Welsh gave Charlton an early lead. Chelsea equalised through centre forward Mills soon afterwards. There was no further score in the first half and, sixteen minutes into the second, the fog that had been creeping over the ground became so thick that the referee was forced to abandon the game. Heavy fog in London in the days before smokeless fuel and clean air legislation was not uncommon but this was no ordinary blanket of gloom. This was the worst Christmas fog since 1904. In a report entitled 'Fog Stops Game but Goalie Didn't Know', the *Daily News* tells of partygoers losing their way, a cross-channel ferry stranded seven hours at sea while trying to find Calais, firemen fighting fires they couldn't see and goalkeeper Bartram left guarding his goal!

The Chelsea programme for the equivalent match early in the 1948/49 season records the incident that will forever be associated with Bartram and 'The Bridge'. 'It was one Christmas time; a crisp and sunny morning. The game had been in progress for some time when, from the direction of Lots Road power station, a bank of fog suddenly appeared and quickly descended like a blanket upon the pitch. It was fantastic – but the game went on as best as possible. Behind each goal spectators lit newspapers that, by some miracle, bearing in mind it was Christmas time and none had been published, they seemed to find from somewhere.' The article mistakenly says the game went on for ninety minutes but let's not let the facts detract from a good story. To continue: 'Back in the Charlton dressing room the players, talking among themselves, suddenly noticed Bartram was missing. "Where's Sam?" asked Don Welsh. Everyone looked blank. Then, as one, it dawned on the Charlton players what had happened. Sam had been left out there in the fog. He had not heard the whistle. He thought the game was still in progress. A search party was sent out. Sam was located in his goal, trying hard to peer through the fog to spot the Chelsea forwards, and the position was explained to him. Sam Bartram laughed "and so to think I was wondering why everything had gone so quiet." So, by walking round the touchlines, using them as a guide, the search party arrived back at the Charlton dressing room.'

Jim Oakes (centre) checks Chelsea forward Jim Argue's progress as Sam gathers.

Two days later there were 51,000 at The Valley for the return game, which did go the distance. Charlton won 3-1 after taking a three-goal interval lead through inside right George Robinson and wingers Harold Hobbis and George Tadman. Fittingly, when the Christmas fixture was replayed in April, it ended as a 1-1 draw. Again Don Welsh was the Charlton goal scorer.

On 1 January Charlton were at Leeds United and still surprising the critics with their continued success. Reporter Allan Cave asked, 'How do they do it? That is what a lot of people ask when they notice that Charlton, a Third Division club at this time three years ago, remain with fewer defeats against their name than any other club in the First Division this season. The answer is a highly systemised defence with a wonder goalkeeper at the back of it all. Bartram did many grand things, but no save was greater than that he made from full-back Sproston, who shot terrifically from an angle forty yards out on the right with his left foot. The ball sped low and true for the far corner of the goal. A score all the way, until Bartram dived and scooped the ball away one-handed. Indeed a masterpiece.'

A *Sunday Pictorial* special was headed, 'THEY SHALL NOT PASS, BARTRAM'S RESOLUTION' and added 'for Charlton, Bartram, as usual, was in dazzling form in goal and he brought off saves which sent the crowd swaying to its feet and earned the applause of both sets of supporters.'

Early in 1938 Sam thought he might be destined for Wembley as Charlton at long last embarked on an FA Cup run. Having overcome Cardiff City 5-0 and Leeds United 2-1 in the third and fourth rounds at home, six-time winners Aston Villa were drawn to meet Charlton at The Valley in the fifth round. Sam recalls that things didn't run well for the team and they were lucky to draw 1-1 in front of the club's all-time record crowd of 75,031. Sam adds, 'The replay at Villa Park on the Wednesday was again a draw, 2-2. This time we were very unfortunate; leading two goals to nil with ten minutes to go, everybody thought it was all over, except the Villa players, who fought back in that great Villa tradition. So we had to fight it out once more, this time at Highbury. This is one match I shall always remember. After twenty minutes' play, things broke about even, then we started an attack on the right wing and eventually the ball was transferred to Harold Hobbis on the left, who raced for goal. As he was about to shoot, Massie, the Villa half-back, went into a split-second tackle. Hobbis went down and by the look on his face we at once knew something tragic had happened. He was carried off on a stretcher and when the whistle blew for half-time with the score 1-0 to us, we all rushed to the dressing room to find out how he was. Harold was lying on the table and the doctor had splints on his injury. We then knew he had broken his leg. Just before we were going out for the second-half, he raised himself up and said "Sorry I can't be with you but good luck lads." Determined to hang onto our lead our boys played like men possessed, and then once again bad luck dogged us. Our centre forward George Tadman got injured and had to go on the right wing. We were struggling hard with nine sound men and holding our slender lead.

FA Cup action and
Charlton's record crowd
v. Aston Villa at The
Valley in February 1938.

Alas, dame fortune was not with us that day and further injury to left half Don
Welsh just about put paid to our chances, but the boys fought on against the odds
and it was not until the final minutes that Aston Villa equalised and went on to
score three further goals and run out 4-1 winners. What took place after the final
whistle will live in my memory forever. The whole of the 60,000 crowd stood up
and cheered us as I have never heard before. A great tribute to a very gallant set of
losers and a great climax to a classic match.'

Charlton Athletic First Division 1937/38. From left to right, back row: Joe Jobling, Bert Turner, Sam Bartram, John Oakes, Don Welsh, George Green. Front row: George Tadman, George Robinson, Jimmy Oakes, Thomas Owens, Les Boulter, Harold Hobbis.

The total attendance figure for the tie between Charlton and Aston Villa was in excess of 200,000, a record that can never be broken as second replays are no longer played. The earlier matches with Cardiff and Leeds attracted a combined attendance of 81,000. Thus nearly 300,000 spectators had seen Charlton's five FA Cup games. With the club finishing in fourth spot in the First Division and conceding just 14 goals at home, they had further enhanced their claim to be considered among the First Division elite.

In the close season Charlton were offered a repeat match with the French national team but instead made a three-match visit to Sweden. Fifteen players made the trip; Sam Bartram, Cyril Blott, Les Boulter, 'Sailor' Brown, George Green, Joe Jobling, Eric Lancelotte, Joe Mallett, James Oakes, John Oakes, George Robinson, Jack Shreeve, Bert Tann, Bert Turner and Monty Wilkinson. They twice met a Swedish representative XI, drawing 1-1 in both Norrkoping and Gothenburg. The third game against AIK Stockholm resulted in a 3-2 victory.

It is significant to note that admission charges to Charlton home games had not increased since the club reached the First Division and terrace fans could cheer on Bartram and his colleagues for 6d and 1s (2.5p and 5p), or for 2s 6d (12.5p) from the comfort of the grandstand. A seat for the season cost just £3.

The new season began with disappointing away defeats at Bolton, Preston, Liverpool and Middlesbrough but as usual The Valley provided better fortune.

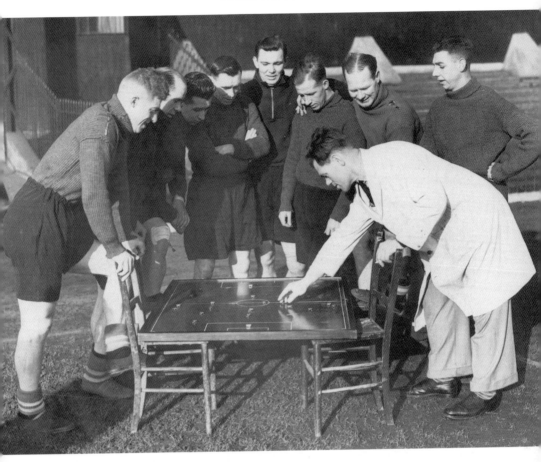

Sam and colleagues receive a tactical briefing from trainer Jimmy Trotter.

The home schedule opened with a Monday afternoon meeting with Stoke City. Sam saved a penalty from Steele after Don Welsh impeded Stanley Matthews and the Addicks won 4-2. Wins over Leeds United and Leicester City continued the run. Then Birmingham City were visitors on one of The Valley's more unusual afternoons. Prime Minister Neville Chamberlain, a Birmingham man himself, was at the match, having recently returned from Munich where, with the politicians fearing possible European conflict, he had met Chancellor Hitler. The Rector of Charlton offered prayers for peace before the game, which ended in a 4-4 draw.

A week later the hitherto poor away form was redressed with a goal in each half in a 2-0 win against Manchester United at Old Trafford, and a successful period for the team was under way. However, when Charlton were next on their travels, at Portsmouth, things proved a little uncomfortable for 'keeper Bartram. Sam had just saved a penalty when, unusually for those days, two players were sent off by the referee. Sections of the home crowd became incensed. Journalist

Bob Finlay records, 'Some decided to wreak their anger on Bartram, the Charlton goalkeeper. First the goal-netting caught fire; later he dropped as if shot when about to take a goal kick. Mr Seed, the Charlton manager, told me afterwards that some "sportsman" had caught Bartram on the head with half a brick.'

The reporter adds, 'There is nothing about the game I want to remember apart from some daring work by Bartram. Charlton, without George Green and Don Welsh, called-up for the England *v.* Wales international match, won 2–0 – the first team to win a First Division match at Fratton Park for a year.' A month later Sam was in the news again, this time for his performance at Blundell Park, Grimsby. A headline and report read, '"HOUDINI" BARTRAM'S GREAT DISPLAY AT GRIMSBY. Sammy Bartram has been called many names in his time, but after his great display at Grimsby on Saturday he earned a new one – "Houdini". That is what the fisher-folk called him at Blundell Park. They just could not understand how he always managed to be just on the right spot. Take two instances; the first was when Grimsby were awarded a free-kick a yard or two outside Charlton's penalty area. The kick was taken by Howe, who has the most wicked left-foot drive in football. An identical kick a few weeks ago left Chelsea's Woodley well nigh paralysed, but Bartram coolly gathered what must have felt like a young cannonball. Then, shortly before the final whistle was blown by Mr Twist, the referee, Bartram left his net unguarded and ran out to the left wing to make a clearance. Alas, he failed and Boyd placed an accurate centre to Bartholomew, who was standing in front of the empty net. Bartram I've said was out on the wing. Bartholomew was in front of the net, so Bartholomew chuckled, and said, "Boys, this is easy!" He let fly, and Bartram, standing in the middle of the opening, saved very calmly. "Well, well, well!" said Mr Bartholomew, or words to that effect. How did Bartram do it? Search me; I'm not a member of the Magic Circle.' The 11,691 who watched the 1–1 draw at Grimsby presumably had no idea either but that's the stuff that creates legends. Incidentally, winger Bartholomew was also Grimsby's scorer that mysterious November afternoon.

On New Year's Eve Charlton were at Elland Road, Leeds, and the Bartram 'magic' was recorded thus, 'Bartram made his best save for years. Wonder goalkeeper Bartram and a bit of bad luck left Leeds United fighting out for a last-minute win against Charlton Athletic. One human-bullet dive, to a shot from Cochrane, was considered the best save seen at Elland Road for years.' Unfortunately Sam couldn't stop the home side claiming the points with a winning goal a minute from time.

Although the season progressed in unpredictable fashion, two notable 'doubles' were achieved. In February Sam saved a penalty at The Valley as Charlton overcame Manchester United 7–1, to complement the earlier success at Old Trafford. Then, in April, Everton, the champions, whose 100 per cent home run had been ended by Charlton with a 4–1 away victory at Goodison Park in December, found Sam in top form as they went down 1–2 at The Valley.

A newspaper headline proclaimed, 'BARTRAM AND RIST DEFIED CHAMPIONS. What a game! Rip roaring from start to finish. The Charlton defence had the worst battering imaginable in the second half and stood up to it in wonderful manner... In attack after attack Bartram performed wonders. Shreeve kicked a ball off the line when it seemed hopeless. Bartram dived to a couple of express shots and saved miraculously at short range... Rist was nearly one half of Charlton and Bartram was his usual self.'

The win over Everton was followed by victories at Stoke and at home to Preston to lift Charlton to third place in the final First Division table, the second time in three seasons of First Division football that they had finished as top London club. It was just reward when Sam Bartram, John Oakes and 'Sailor' Brown were selected to join the Football Association party to tour South Africa that summer.

Apart from playing in an international trial, this was Sam's first major honour as a professional and it was a very excited Bartram who set sail from Southampton on 11 May, aboard the *Athlone Castle*, just four days after the end of the season. Eighteen players made up the FA party to South Africa in 1939: George Ainsley (Leeds United), Harry Betmead (Grimsby Town), Sam Bartram (Charlton Athletic), Pat Beasley (Huddersfield Town), Cliff Britton (Everton), Eric Brook (Manchester City), Albert 'Sailor' Brown (Charlton Athletic), Ted Fenton (West Ham United), Micky Fenton (Middlesbrough), Lester Finch (Barnet), Ken Gadsby (Leeds United), Jack Gibbons (Brentford & RAF), George Jackson (Everton), Johnny Jones (Everton), Jim Lewis (Walthamstow Avenue), John Mahon (Huddersfield Town), Johnny Mapson (Sunderland) and John Oakes (Charlton Athletic). The Football Association officials accompanying the group were Messrs C. Wreford-Brown, H. Hughes and A. Stollery (trainer). Wing half Cliff Britton, centre half Harry Betmead, wingers Pat Beasley and Eric Brook and centre forward Micky Fenton were all full internationals. Brook had previously scored 10 times in 18 appearances for England. Three of the players, Finch, Lewis and Gibbons, were amateurs.

The voyage to Cape Town took fourteen days. The party amused themselves with various sporting pursuits and even formed a choir and entertained their fellow passengers. In South Africa 12 games were played at three and four-day intervals between 27 May and 5 July, including 3 Test matches. The tour started at Cape Town and the party travelled thousands of miles via East London, Johannesburg (three times), Benoni, Durban (twice), Pietermaritzburg, Bloemfontein and Pretoria, to Kimberley. Sam shared the goalkeeping duties with Johnny Mapson of Sunderland, playing 6 games each. Remarkably the two Fentons, Ted and Micky, played in eleven of the fixtures, including all three Tests. The latter was top scorer with 24 goals. Ted's younger brother Benny, a postwar signing from Millwall, later became Charlton captain.

The name Bartram made its first appearance on an 'international' teamsheet when Sam kept goal in the first Test match of the tour at The Wanderers Ground,

FA touring team to South Africa 1939. From left to right, back row: G. Jackson (Everton), S. Bartram (Charlton Athletic), K. Gadsby (Leeds United), J. Mapson (Sunderland), J. Jones (Everton). Middle row: H. Hughes (FA), J. Lewis (Walthamstow Avenue), C. Britton (Everton), J. Oakes (Charlton Athletic), A. Stollery (Trainer), H. Betmead (Grimsby Town), E. Fenton (West Ham United), A. Hemming (S.A. Manager). Seated: J. Mahon (Huddersfield Town), G. Ainsley (Leeds United), M. Fenton (Middlesbrough), C. Wreford-Brown (FA), A. Gibbons (RAF), A. Brown (Charlton Athletic), L. Finch (Barnet). Front row: A. Beasley (Huddersfield Town), E. Brook (Manchester City, Captain).

Johannesburg on 17 June. The teams that day were: South Africa: E.C. Van Vuuren; R.J. Diers, A.J. Hughes; R. Gibson (all Southern Transvaal), L.E. Graham, W.E. Lawson; D. Wilson, W. Davidson (all Eastern Transvaal), T.A. Mitchell, E.H. Smethurst (both Natal), W. Sloan (Eastern Transvaal). England XI: Sam Bartram; George Jackson, Jack Jones; Cliff Britton, John Oakes, Ted Fenton; Pat Beasley, Jim Lewis, Micky Fenton, 'Sailor' Brown, Eric Brook (Captain). The England XI won 3-0 with inside left Lewis scoring twice and centre forward Fenton once. A report on the tour by Roy Fairfax in *The Footballer* magazine of 1939 says, 'The score would certainly have been greater had Van Vuuren not made several spectacular saves. In contrast, the red-haired English goalkeeper Bartram had a relatively easy introduction to international football.'

Sam recalls, 'The standard of football played in South Africa was very good... it wasn't easy, especially against their national eleven. Also bad were the climatic conditions; sometimes we played at 3,000 feet above sea level and it was difficult to get one's breath. Also the heat at times was 90° in the shade. So you see how difficult it was for us.'

South Africa bound. From left to right: John Mahon, Jack Gibbons, Sam Bartram and John Oakes.

The tour was a great success both on and off the field. In terms of results, eleven wins and a single-goal defeat against Southern Transvaal at Johannesburg, on a bone-hard ground at high altitude, speaks for itself. The one early setback gave the South African football public encouragement for the Test series and record gates were recorded. However, the English team were victorious in the two international matches played at Johannesburg and the other at Durban.

The FA's official report of the tour is glowing in its plaudits for the tourists. 'No praise is too high for the conduct of the touring players. It was acclaimed both in the press and by those with whom they came in contact, including managers of hotels where the party stayed. It is much to be hoped that the Football Association will, in making their selection of players for international matches, continue the practice of taking into consideration the reputation of each individual for decency and good sportsmanship.'

Of the goalkeepers it adds. 'BARTRAM and MAPSON. Goalkeeping was perfectly safe in the hands of either of these players. Neither could be faulted and both are worthy of international caps.' The report summarises the performances of Sam's club colleagues thus: 'OAKES: Played his usual third back game very well. It seems a pity, however, that he is excluded from exploiting the qualities of the complete footballer, which he would seem to possess. BROWN: Combines a conscientious desire to give of his best and be ready to help the defence with dribbling powers that would be more effective if his work was not so often marred by a poor finish.'

Off-the-field hospitality was warm and friendly and the tourists managed sightseeing trips to enjoy the splendid views from Cape Town's Table Mountain and to the Kruger National Park game reserve. The party stayed overnight in a lonely mountain retreat on the way to the park, just before the first international match with South Africa at Johannesburg, but that night big game took on a different meaning. It was basic accommodation, with players sleeping on mattresses on the floor. Sam, writing in the *Sunday People* years later, recalls a sleepless night. 'I had just dozed off when – thump! – there was a bump on the door. I awoke with a start and then came a noise like roaring and growling. Those old red locks of mine began to stand on end. "Lions", I thought immediately, and lay listening. Pat Beasley, the Arsenal and Huddersfield winger woke next. "Just hark at those ruddy dogs, Sam," he said. "Barking all the time. How those other blokes can sleep through it I just don't know." But the others weren't to lie dreaming long. Soon there came more bumps. More roars. More growls. Soon every one of us was awake and listening. Most of the boys took Beasley's view, that the hotel manager's four big Alsatians had been shut out and were yelping and scratching at the door to come in. But Eric Brook and George Ainsley agreed with Uncle Sammy; "Lions it must be." For an hour or more we lay there wondering and arguing whether we should let the dogs in – or whether we might become big cats' meat if we tried to. Finally we could stand it no longer. We sent for the manager. "Can't you keep your bloomin' dogs quiet?" asked Ted Fenton. "Dogs!" replied the manager. "They're not dogs, they're lions. They'll keep this up till dawn. Nothing to worry about." But eighteen intrepid English footballers, eighteen usually brave forwards and defenders – not to mention this goalkeeper! – determined that they too would await the dawn wide awake just in case! And the hotel manager gave us the comfort of a gun in our bedroom, also just in case!'

The England squad on parade in South Africa. Sam is third from left.

Sam in action in Durban.

Back home the story must have raised many laughs as Sam and his colleagues prepared for the new season, which began on 26 August away to Stoke. Two goals in each half from the home side inflicted a heavy defeat. At The Valley Charlton overcame Leeds United 1-0 in midweek, then accounted for Manchester United 2-0 at the weekend, but all was in vain for, the following day, just twelve months after Prime Minister Chamberlain's appearance at Charlton, war was declared and the 1939/40 Football League programme was abandoned, The Valley closed and players' contracts were cancelled.

three

WARTIME

Hostilities had seemed inevitable for some time, so much so that in April 1939 a Football Association circular had encouraged footballers to become role models for the country's youth by joining voluntary organisations. Following the outbreak of war Sam spent a period in the War Reserve Police. This meant he was available to play for Charlton in the makeshift South Regional League that sprung into action in late October.

Wartime football was a popular entertainment during these dark days and although attendances were well below those in peacetime, most clubs fielded teams and were comparatively well supported. With so many players serving in the armed forces a flexible approach was adopted, with 'guest' appearances permitted. As several league clubs suffered bomb damage or wartime closure, there was also a compromise over grounds. Among the temporarily groundless clubs were Millwall, who shared The Valley, Manchester United, who played home matches at Manchester City's Maine Road stadium and Arsenal, whose temporary home was at White Hart Lane, Tottenham.

In fact, it was at White Hart Lane against Arsenal that Charlton began their wartime schedule. Although attempts were made to resemble normality, the results of the early games indicate a distinctly unreal flavour. Arsenal beat Charlton 8-4, with Leslie Compton scoring four goals, three of them from the penalty spot. The next 2 matches, both at The Valley, saw the Addicks win 8-1 against Southend and then repeat the score a week later against Clapton Orient. A 4–3 win over Crystal Palace followed at Selhurst Park.

Bartram was in goal for the first sixteen outings of the 1939/40 wartime campaign but afterwards his appearances were restricted, having enlisted in the Royal Air Force as a physical training instructor. Sam was posted to the RAF's PT headquarters at Uxbridge, Middlesex, in January 1940. Among his fellow recruits were Arsenal's Jack Crayston, Ted Drake, Alf Kirchen, George Marks and Laurie Scott, Vic Buckingham of Tottenham, Gilbert Glidden from Reading and Surrey cricketers Tom Barling, Bob Gregory, Jack Parker and Stan Squires.

Sam recalls, 'Going into the services was quite a change from what I had been used to and I never thought I would ever settle down at all, but after a few days I realised that I had to make a go of it, so I just took the bull by the horns and everything turned out alright.' Due to the emergencies of wartime and the shortage of PT instructors, what was normally a three-month training course was crammed into one hectic month. The recruits were taught physical training, class teaching, anatomy and physiology. Sam was on parade at 8 a.m. and finished training at 5 p.m., then was required to spend the evening studying until 'lights out'.

Sam adds, 'I must say I really enjoyed it; the work was hard and I never thought one could learn so much in such a short time.' At the end of the course he was awarded a certificate and given the rank of corporal. Bartram's initial posting was to Derby and he played twice as a guest for nearby Notts County. His outings for the Meadow Lane club were limited, as Sam was soon transferred to the North-West, initially to Padgate and then to West Kirby. In the meantime he played for Charlton whenever possible, making a total of 26 appearances during the season.

Like other clubs Charlton also relied on guests during the Second World War and their line-up in a 3-1 Regional League victory at Portsmouth in March 1940 is worth recording: Swift (Manchester City); Turner, Wright; Tann, John Oakes, Ford; Lancelotte, Brown, Lawton (Everton), Welsh, Thomas (Brentford). It was England goalkeeper Frank Swift's only game in Charlton colours, whereas international centre forward Tommy Lawton played twice, having been a colleague of Bartram's in a 3-2 home win over Brentford the previous weekend.

For Sam, who a few months earlier had made his international debut on tour in South Africa, it had been a disjointed season, as indeed it was for most other players. However, April 1940 brought a special highlight with his selection for England's first wartime international at Wembley. Despite the war, home international matches continued and, although no caps were awarded, the games were popular with players and football followers and helped to bring a semblance of normality to the sporting scene. England had already met Wales twice since the outbreak of war, at Wrexham and Cardiff in November, followed by a meeting with Scotland at St James' Park, Newcastle, in December.

On Saturday 13 April a crowd of 40,000 saw Wales' first appearance at Wembley, when the teams were: England: Sam Bartram (Charlton Athletic); Joe Bacuzzi (Fulham), Eddie Hapgood (Arsenal, Captain); Ken Willingham (Huddersfield Town), Stan Cullis (Wolverhampton Wanderers), Wilf Copping (Leeds United); Stanley Matthews (Stoke City), Willie Hall (Tottenham Hotspur), Dennis Westcott (Wolverhampton Wanderers), Len Goulden (West Ham United), Denis Compton (Arsenal). Wales: Cyril Sidlow (Wolverhampton Wanderers); Bert Turner (Charlton Athletic), George Williams (Millwall); George Green (Charlton Athletic), Robert Davies (Nottingham Forest), Douglas Witcomb (West Bromwich Albion); Idris Hopkins (Brentford), Don Dearson (Birmingham City), Dai Astley (Blackpool), Bryn Jones (Arsenal), Leslie Jones (Arsenal).

Right: On RAF duty with
Arsenal and England centre
forward Ted Drake (centre).

Below: An off-duty snow
fight with wife Helen and
sister-in-law Alice.

This is how the official programme introduced Sam's first Wembley appearance. 'SAM BARTRAM (Charlton Athletic) – Goalkeeper. Spectacular red-headed Sam Bartram became a goalkeeper through accident. At school and in junior soccer he was a left half; then he became a centre forward with a goal-scoring reputation. On the eve of an important cup tie his club's goalkeeper was injured. Although without experience Sam agreed to keep goal, remained there and was recommended to Charlton. Came south on two months' trial. Did not impress until his last match when he was signed as a professional in November 1934. Helped Charlton go from Third to First Division in successive seasons, and has missed only 4 games in last four campaigns. Toured South Africa last year. A corporal instructor in the RAF, he passed his course with high marks.'

Despite England's 0–1 defeat, Sam was selected for England's next game, in May, against Scotland at Hampden Park, Glasgow but, with the RAF on alert, his unit was recalled and Vic Woodley of Chelsea was detailed to take the overnight train north. This was a double disappointment for the Charlton 'keeper who, on reporting for service duty, was received with surprise by his commanding officer, who fully expected him to be in Glasgow!

The following season, 1940/41, Sam was stationed up north and appeared regularly for Liverpool, playing 16 matches, including the first 10 games of the season. In the Liverpool team were two of Anfield's all time greats', Scottish winger Billy Liddell and later manager supreme Bob Paisley, from Hetton-le-Hole in County Durham, close to Bartram country.

In February 1941 came another England call-up, this time against Scotland, for the first international of the season at St James' Park, Newcastle, familiar territory for Sam. There were 25,000 at Gallowgate to see England lose 2–3 to their oldest rivals. The line-ups were: England: Bartram (Charlton Athletic); Bacuzzi (Fulham), Mountford (Huddersfield Town); Willingham (Huddersfield Town), Cullis (Wolverhampton Wanderers, Captain), Mercer (Everton); Birkett (Newcastle United), Mannion (Middlesbrough), Lawton (Everton), Goulden (West Ham United), Hanson (Chelsea). Scotland; Dawson (Rangers); Hogg (Celtic), A. Beattie (Preston North End); McDonald (Celtic), Dykes (Heart of Midlothian), G. Brown (Rangers); Milne (Middlesbrough), Walker (Heart of Midlothian), J. Smith (Rangers), Wallace (Clyde), Caskie (Everton). England scored through Ralph Birkett and Tommy Lawton. Doug Wallace netted twice for Scotland as the teams shared a four-goal first half. Unfortunately for England and Sam, a back-headed own goal, late in the game, swung things Scotland's way.

Later in the season the RAF posted Sam to Bournemouth, where he helped to train Canadian fliers and played as a guest for the local club. Having the England goalkeeper in their side was a big boost for Boscombe and, despite restrictions on news, due to wartime sensitivities on the South Coast, his first appearance on 22 March was heralded by the *Bournemouth Daily Echo*, 'Bartram Playing for Boscombe. Boscombe have attractive visitors to Dean Court tomorrow in

Portsmouth, who will field a very strong side. Boscombe will have Bartram, the famous Charlton and England goalkeeper in their side.

Their report of the game states: 'FINE VICTORY. Boscombe Have Good Day. Pompey Concede Three Goals. It was fitting that the biggest crowd which has passed the turnstiles at Dean Court this season should have been present on the ground on Saturday, when Boscombe scored their best victory over a star-studded Portsmouth side by three clear goals. The win coincided with the first appearance of "Sam" Bartram, the Charlton and England goalkeeper, and no doubt his presence had a tonic effect on the players in front of him. It also probably had the effect of swelling the "gate" for Bartram is a spectacular player, apart from being in the first flight. He has a pair of vice-like hands and although called upon only two or three times to really exert himself he showed how good he can be. If Bartram plays regularly, as it is hoped he will, better times should be ahead of Boscombe.'

Sam played 5 times for the club that season, before being a member of the winning England team against Wales at Ninian Park, Cardiff, in June. The teams on that occasion were: Wales: Sidlow (Wolverhampton Wanderers); Hughes (Birmingham City), Turner (Charlton Athletic); Dearson (Birmingham City), T.G. Jones (Everton), Witcomb (West Bromwich Albion); Rogers (Swansea Town), Woodward (Fulham), James (Cardiff City), B. Jones (Arsenal), L. Jones (Arsenal). England: Bartram (Charlton Athletic), Bacuzzi (Fulham), Hapgood (Arsenal, Captain); Britton (Everton), Cullis (Wolverhampton Wanderers), Buckingham (Tottenham Hotspur); Kirchen (Arsenal), Hagan (Sheffield United), Welsh (Charlton Athletic), Goulden (West Ham United), Finch (Barnet). England won 3-2 before a 20,000 attendance, with two goals from Jimmy Hagan and the other scored by Sam's good friend and Charlton colleague Don Welsh.

August 1941 saw Bartram back in goal for Charlton at the start of the London League season. His last appearance had been at Southampton in June 1940. His RAF commitments, however, limited him to 15 Charlton matches, mostly during the early and late stages of the season. Guest outings were also restricted to 2 each for Crystal Palace and Bournemouth and 1 for Brentford. Both matches for Bournemouth, who only played for part of the year, were in the Football League War Cup and resulted in a win over Cardiff City and defeat by Southampton. At Bournemouth in February, the local newspaper records a 2-1 win for the home team but reports, 'Cardiff were the better side, and had it not been for a distinguished performance by Bartram, the Charlton Athletic goalkeeper, between the posts and vigorous and unflagging work by the Boscombe defence generally, Boscombe would have most certainly have been in arrears at the interval.'

Exactly a month later, Sam was on cup duty for Bournemouth at Southampton. Again one goal was the difference between the teams but this time in favour of the Saints. The *Bournemouth Daily Echo* observed, 'The visiting defence tackled and kicked in dour determination, but there would have been more than one goal against them had not Bartram kept goal superbly, cutting out centres and positioning himself so that he made goalkeeping look easy.'

After fifteen months of RAF service on the South Coast came a posting to Harrogate, North Yorkshire, and a connection that was to play a large part in Sam's later career. He was soon in action for York City, making his debut in October 1942 in a 4-3 home win over Newcastle, in which guest Frank O'Donnell of Aston Villa scored all four goals. At York Sam teamed up with Charlton colleagues 'Sailor' Brown and Tommy Dawson and played 22 games in his first term with the club. He also made 1 appearance each for Bradford City, Birmingham City and West Ham in 1942/43, in addition to a couple of early season games for Charlton.

Sam clearly enjoyed his time at Bootham Crescent and became a favourite of the York City supporters, and how the crowds turned out that season after the team finished seventeenth out of forty-seven in League North during the first half of the season! Then, with six wins and a draw from nine League North War Cup qualifying games, they reached the competition proper. In round one a 2-3 reverse in the first leg at Newcastle was wiped out by a 2-0 home victory. Home and away wins over Bradford City, who included future England internationals Len Shackleton and Billy Elliott – both to become Sunderland stars – were followed by a double success against Chesterfield. All these matches drew five-figure attendances, with the away semi-final leg at Sheffield Wednesday attracting 35,253 to Hillsborough. Unfortunately York went down 0-3 but salvaged their pride before a wartime record 16,350 fans in the home leg, with a 1-1 draw. Sam, in fact, missed out on two cup finals that spring, having been one game away with York and unavailable for Charlton, who won through to the southern cup final, against Arsenal, at Wembley.

The following season 1943/44 Sam managed 4 Football League South matches for Charlton, two in October and one each in December and January but regularly appeared for York, playing 30 times. This time he was denied a cup run with his adopted club when York went out to Bradford City in the northern knock-out stages but late in the season was called south by Charlton, who had reached the semi-final of the Football League (South) Cup. Bartram was in the team on All Fools' Day at Stamford Bridge against a Tottenham Hotspur side weakened by calls for an Army v. RAF match in Edinburgh. Nevertheless, just fewer than 35,000 spectators witnessed Charlie Revell and Bill Robinson score three goals between them to steer Charlton to a second successive Wembley final.

A fortnight later and almost exactly four years after his Wembley debut for England, Sam returned to the 'twin towers' with Charlton, to meet Chelsea and play in his first final since keeping goal for Boldon Villa against Tyne Dock (Pymans) at Stanley Street, South Shields, ten eventful years earlier. The night before the match, full of excitement and expectation, he dreamed that Chelsea went into the lead but Charlton fought back to win. That was precisely what happened! Joe Payne put Chelsea ahead through an early penalty. Charlie Revell equalised within five minutes, then two goals in two minutes by skipper Don Welsh and a second from Revell, both set up by winger Chris Duffy, gave Charlton a 3-1 advantage at half-time. There were no goals for the 85,000 crowd after the break, when the Addicks' defence stood firm in the face of the Chelsea attack and a delighted Sam followed Don Welsh up the steps to the Royal Box, as Charlton's captain received the cup from America's wartime commander, General Dwight D. Eisenhower.

Both final teams relied on guest players. Charlton included wing half Allenby Chilton of Manchester United and wingers Bill Robinson from Sunderland and Chris Duffy of Leith Athletic, a Scottish club from Edinburgh. Chelsea fielded eight outsiders, including Middlesbrough full-back George Hardwick, who was to become England's postwar captain and Manchester United winger Charlie Mitten. The full line-ups were: Charlton Athletic: Bartram; Shreeve, Jobling; Smith, John Oakes, Chilton (Manchester U); W. Robinson (Sunderland), Brown, Revell, Welsh, Duffy (Leith Athletic). Chelsea: Woodley; Hardwick (Middlesbrough), Westwood (Manchester City); Russell (Airdrieonians), Harris (Wolverhampton Wanderers), Foss; L. Ashcroft (Tranmere Rovers), Fagan (Liverpool), Payne, Bowie (Aberdeen), Mitten (Manchester United). Charlton marked the win by presenting the match ball to Joe Jobling, their longest-serving player.

A month later on 20 May, unchanged Charlton met Aston Villa, the Football League (North) Cup winners in a charity match at Stamford Bridge. The teams fought out a 1-1 draw, in a high-class display, in front of a near-39,000 crowd. Charlie Revell was the Addicks' scorer. Both clubs were awarded a trophy.

Sam watches Don Welsh receive the wartime Football League (South) Cup from General Dwight D. Eisenhower at Wembley in 1944.

Sam was soon back at York and his games for Charlton the following season were limited to a 7-1 win at Brighton in November, a 4-0 conquest of Clapton Orient on Christmas Day 1944, defeats at Brentford and Luton in January and March and a 5-3 victory over Fulham at Craven Cottage in May 1945. In between times he made single guest appearances for Bradford City and Crewe Alexandra, along with 23 outings for York City.

Sam will always be remembered at York for a couple of cup exploits that season. In a League North War Cup win against Bradford in March he scored from the penalty spot. A month later he went one better, scoring both City's goals from penalties in the 2-0 Tyne, Wear & Tees Cup victory over Darlington. Malcolm Huntington, the chief sports writer of the *Evening Press*, who as a lad was inspired to take up goalkeeping after watching Bartram from the terraces at Bootham Crescent, recalls, 'He ran up from a distance and fired unstoppable shots high into the net.'

In between these scoring feats had come an approach from Millwall manager Jack Cock, the former England centre forward, to assist the Lions, who had reached the semi-final of the Football League (South) Cup but were short of a regular goalkeeper. Sam teamed up with Charlton's south London neighbours for their semi-final with Arsenal. A 1-0 victory took Millwall to Wembley for the first time. It was a great day for the New Cross club renowned for their FA Cup exploits, having reached the semi-final three times, more recently in 1937 and twice previously, as a non-league force, in the early 1900s.

In April, for the second year running, the name of Bartram figured on a cup final team sheet against Chelsea, as did that of his Charlton and York City teammate 'Sailor' Brown. A total of only ten regular players were on view to the 90,000 who packed Wembley. The teams, who were introduced to King George VI on the pitch before the game were: Millwall: Bartram (Charlton Athletic); Dudley, G. Fisher; Ludford (Tottenham Hotspur), E. Smith, Tyler; Rawlings, R. Brown (Charlton Athletic), Jinks, T. Brown, Williams (Aberdeen). Chelsea: Black (Aberdeen); Winter (Bolton Wanderers), Hardwick (Middlesbrough); Russell, Harris (Wolverhampton Wanderers), Foss; Wardle (Exeter City), L. Smith (Brentford), Payne, Goulden (West Ham United), McDonald (Bournemouth). There were no substitutes in those days, so neutral Willie Hurrell, who later joined Millwall, was reserve for both teams. Sam kept a clean sheet in a goal-less first half to add to his unbeaten second half twelve months earlier, but was unable to stop guest wingers Wardle and McDonald scoring later in the game to win the cup for Chelsea.

This was a disappointment for Sam and Millwall but there was better, more significant, news on the horizon. That summer the Second World War drew towards a close after six years of conflict. So it was a relieved RAF Sergeant Bartram who shed his uniform and headed back to The Valley, yet it took another year before league football was revived on a national basis. The 1945/46 season

In goal as a guest for Millwall in the 1945 wartime Wembley final.

was a period of transition, with Football League clubs restricted to regional con-
tests as they were in wartime, but with the added spice of the FA Challenge Cup
competition, which had not been contested since Portsmouth beat Wolves 4-1 at
Wembley in April 1939.

four

CUP GLORY

For Charlton supporters who had been serving away from home during the Second World War, it must have been reassuring to see their favourite goalkeeper back in the green jersey when the club embarked on the new season. It started brightly with four straight wins, then, significantly, Sam missed the next game – his only absence all term – and the run ended. However, a subsequent unbeaten spell of 19 matches followed, stretching into the new year and putting Charlton in line for league honours.

Elsewhere the focus of attention had been on the Moscow Dynamos, a touring team from Russia. They attracted huge crowds and much publicity. Their first match at Stamford Bridge was played with 85,000 spectators in the ground, some on the roof of the stand and thousands of others stranded outside. Everyone was keen to see these postwar tourists. Sam was at Tottenham for Moscow Dynamos' match with Arsenal, when at half-time he heard a request announced for a deputy goalkeeper. Wyn Griffiths of Cardiff City, one of several guest players drafted in by Arsenal, was unable to continue after receiving a kick on the head. Sam hot-footed it to the dressing room to find Harry Brown, the Queens Park Rangers 'keeper, had arrived ahead of him and already been recruited for the second half. Three days later the Dynamos' players were watching Sam. They were among the spectators at Charlton's 4-2 victory over Fulham at Craven Cottage.

Coincidentally, Fulham and Bartram came face to face four times that season. With the FA Cup restored and played on a home and away two-leg basis, Fulham were Charlton's opponents when they entered at the third round stage. First-leg goals by Chris Duffy, Les Fell and Don Welsh set-up a 3-1 advantage going into the second match, which Fulham won 2-1, but the higher aggregate score saw the Addicks through. Duffy and Fell were again on the scoresheet in the fourth and fifth rounds, firstly against Wolves, who Charlton overcame 5-2 and 1-1, and then after a 1-1 stalemate at Deepdale, in a 6-0 win over Preston at The Valley – with 50,000 present on a midweek afternoon.

Bartram and company were now in uncharted territory, having taken the club beyond the fifth round of the FA Cup for the first time. Brentford were duly beaten 6-3 and 3-1 in the sixth round to set up a semi-final with Bolton at Villa Park. The attendance for the match at the famous old Birmingham ground was 70,000 and goals either side of half-time by winger Chris Duffy resulted in a 2-0 victory and much celebration both in the ground and back home in London. Charlton had reached the FA Cup final.

During the cup run league form dwindled, but reaching Wembley clearly gave the team added confidence. From ten league fixtures sandwiched between the semi-final and final, they recorded five wins and three draws, including a 2-1 success against cup final rivals Derby, just a week before the big occasion. Charlton were now riding high in the league and Sam was back at Wembley for a third successive final. The teams, who were introduced to His Majesty King George VI before kick-off, on Saturday 27 April 1946 were: Charlton Athletic: Sam Bartram; Harold Phipps, Jack Shreeve; Bert Turner, John Oakes, Bert Johnson; Les Fell, 'Sailor' Brown, Arthur Turner, Don Welsh (Captain), Chris Duffy. Derby County: Vic Woodley; Jack Nicholas (Captain), Jack Howe; Jim Bullions, Leon Leuty, Chick Musson; Reg Harrison, Raich Carter, Jack Stamps, Peter Docherty, Dally Duncan. It was the second time in two years that the respective goalkeepers had been in opposing teams at Wembley – Woodley had kept goal for Chelsea in 1944.

Charlton failed to find top form both during the goal-less first half and afterwards. Then, ten minutes from time, a shot by Derby winger Duncan was accidentally deflected past the helpless Bartram by colleague Bert Turner to put County ahead. Turner responded immediately with a free kick from outside the Derby penalty area that clipped Docherty as it flew goalwards past Woodley and into the net to level the scores and take the game into extra time. Bert Turner was the first player to score for both sides in an FA Cup final and remarkably both goals came within a minute. Unfortunately for Charlton they were unable to add to their total and Derby eased ahead in extra time to win 4-1.

The match might not have lasted so long without a piece of smart thinking by Sam. With the score at 0-0, he fielded a shot from burly Derby centre forward Jack Stamps and noticed that the ball had deflated. The quick-witted 'keeper then threw the soft ball as far as he could towards the touchline before the referee stopped play, thus avoiding a bounce-up with a new ball in the danger zone, right in front of the Charlton goal.

One member of the Charlton contingent who was able to take some solace from the result at Wembley was Sam Bartram's next door neighbour George Stephenson, the former Derby, Charlton and England forward. The Stephenson household in Blackheath was full of Derby supporters on the eve of the final. George's daughter Jean recalls, 'The night before the match our house in Blackheath was bursting with visitors, all from Derby, who were staying there, and everyone was rooting for Derby. I stayed at my friend Pat's house (George Robinson's daughter) for

Punching away danger in the 1946 FA Cup final.

the night as my room was taken. Mum and all the players' wives had been up to London to get their new outfits for Wembley. I can still see mum in hers, matching dress and coat and, of course, a lovely hat to co-ordinate. Most of the ladies wore hats then. The Charlton team went to a London hotel after the game with wives and officials for a banquet. I remember dad saying he was sorry Charlton had lost, but was happy it was to his old pals at Derby.'

In the three remaining league games, which were squeezed into the week after the cup final, the Addicks lost again to Derby at the Baseball Ground and drew at home with Birmingham and Wolves, finishing third in the league, just one point behind the winners Birmingham City and runners-up Aston Villa. Ironically, the outcome may have been different had Sam not missed a penalty in the league match with Birmingham at St Andrews earlier in the season. With Charlton losing 0-1, skipper Don Welsh, having heard about Bartram the wartime penalty ace from York, invited Sam to add to his tally. The ball was placed on the spot and, after a long run-up, Sam blasted the ball against the crossbar and into orbit. Luckily the ball rebounded high enough for him to scamper back towards goal before Birmingham could mount a counterattack!

After the league schedule ended, Charlton headed for the continent, their first postwar venture abroad. They claimed a notable scalp by beating Racing Club de Paris 6-2 at Colombes Stadium, which had been the focal point of the Olympic Games a couple of decades earlier – *Chariots of Fire* et al. There seemed no limit to the goal scoring prowess of the team of '46 when they followed up with a short tour in Sweden.

Cup and league games had produced 121 goals from 52 matches, with Arthur Turner scoring 34 times and Don Welsh 30. The goal rush continued in France and Sweden. Five matches on the continent brought 24 goals. The players on the Swedish tour were: Sam Bartram, Peter Croker, Tommy Dawson, John Dryden, Chris Duffy, Bert Johnson, Harold Phipps, Charlie Revell, Bill Robinson, George Robinson, Jack Shreeve, Maurice Tadman, Arthur Turner, Bert Turner and Don Welsh. The first game against Swedish League and Cup winners Norrkoping finished 2-2, followed by a 7-7 draw against AIK Stockholm and then wins over Jonkoping 5-3 and Malmo 4-3. Charlton's defence, which had conceded on average just over one goal a game throughout the season, became uncustomarily generous overseas.

When the Football League returned to pre-war proportions in August 1946, the schedule for the abandoned 1939/40 season was reinstituted. In the opening fixtures Charlton found themselves away to Stoke City and Leeds United, then home to Manchester United, just as they had six years earlier. Don Welsh scored in 6 of the first 7 games in the club's mixed start to the new era. Before their first FA Cup tie in January, Charlton recorded only 7 successes in 24 outings. Happily, the cup was to bring the best out of the team.

In the third round at home to Rochdale, a goal-less first half was turned into a 3-0 victory when Chris Duffy, twice, and Eric Lancelotte saw the Addicks home. A fortnight later at The Hawthorns, second-half goals by Duffy and Bill Robinson swung things Charlton's way after West Bromwich Albion had taken the lead. Back home at The Valley in the fifth round, it took a last-minute strike

Charlton Athletic, First Division 1946/47. From left to right, back row: Charlie Revell, Bert Johnson, Harold Phipps, Sam Bartram, Frank Rist, Jack Shreeve, Harold Hobbis, Jimmy Trotter (Trainer). Front row: Bill Robinson, Eric Lancelotte, John Oakes, George Robinson, Chris Duffy.

by Tommy Dawson to clinch a 1-0 win over Blackburn Rovers and a place in the sixth round. Here rivalry was renewed with Preston North End who, after their 0-6 defeat in the fifth round just a year before, were determined to make amends. They did and a goal apiece from wingers Chris Duffy and Gordon Hurst was just enough for Charlton to squeeze through 2-1.

On paper, the result of the semi-final at Leeds seems as if it must have been an easy affair, but this was not the case. Not only did opponents Newcastle United boost an illustrious forward line that included Len Shackleton, Roy Bentley and Jackie Milburn but, before the game, Sam and half the team were suffering from food poisoning. The fact that Charlton lead 3-0 at the interval and went on to win the match 4-0 is truly amazing.

Prior to the match the team was training at Harrogate and several players suffered adverse effects from food they had eaten. The night before the semi-final Dr Montgomery, who as usual was travelling with the party, did his best to cure the ailments, while Jimmy Seed strived to keep the news of his invalids from reaching the press and Charlton's opponents. In his autobiography Sam recalls, 'The last thing our manager wanted was that the supremely confident Newcastle side should know that they would be playing a team of semi-invalids. Nobody watching us play that day, however, would have guessed that a few hours earlier we had been writhing in acute pain. Some little time after the match had started, and just as I was about to take a goal kick, the pain hit me again. I thought I was going to be sick, and I was almost doubled up as the referee, seeing my plight, called on trainer Jimmy Trotter. Jimmy told me to roll up my jersey, and when I did so, he slapped a hot poultice onto my chest and stomach. "That'll cure you, Sam," he said grimly; and he was right. The hotter I got, the more the poultice burned – but it eased the griping pain considerably.'

Such was the intensity of the game and the sickness that skipper Don Welsh, who scored two of the first-half goals, collapsed unconscious in the dressing room after the final whistle. A few days later, now with a clean bill of health, ten of the same team lined-up at The Valley for a league game. Any hangovers were dispelled in the first minute, when Bartram saved a penalty kick taken by Middlesbrough's 'golden boy' Wilf Mannion. The game ended in a 3-3 draw. Three of Charlton's 5 matches leading up to the FA Cup final finished all square.

Saturday 26 April 1947, another year, another Wembley final. A crowd of 98,215 fans were present for the first London v. Lancashire meeting since the inaugural Wembley final of 1923. Charlton met Burnley, who had accounted for high-flying Liverpool in their semi-final and were about to be promoted from the Second Division. The team line-ups were: Charlton Athletic: Sam Bartram; Peter Croker, Jack Shreeve; Bert Johnson, Harold Phipps, Bill Whittaker; Gordon Hurst, Tommy Dawson, Bill Robinson, Don Welsh (Captain), Chris Duffy. Burnley: Jimmy Strong; Arthur Woodruff, Harold Mather; Reg Attwell, Alan Brown (Captain), George Bray; Jackie Chew, Billy Morris, Ray Harrison, Harry Potts, Peter Kippax.

The Addicks fielded six of the previous season's Wembley team, giving them an advantage in experience that proved a key factor. Several Burnley players were unable to live up to their reputations on the big occasion. Defences were on top but the game didn't lack excitement. Harry Potts, later a famous Burnley manager, struck the Charlton bar with a fierce shot and there were last-ditch efforts by Bill Whittaker of Charlton and Harold Mather of Burnley, who successfully cleared their lines to keep the scoresheet blank.

The *Daily Mail* records, 'The Charlton defence, which carried the side through to the final, I cannot fault. Phipps, Croker and Johnson were perhaps outstanding. Bartram made two typical saves; Shreeve was never flurried, while young Billy Whittaker, after being nursed for the first half-hour, did a grand job. An extra word for Croker. He not only played England winger Kippax out of the game, but showed the class that stamps him as a coming international. He was never in

A spectacular save in the 1947 cup final.

Charlton skipper Don Welsh
proudly holds the FA Cup while
Sam waits to receive his medal.

trouble, and his positional play rendered ineffective the speed of his immediate opponent.'

Burnley created most chances but Charlton looked more menacing, particularly with centre forward Bill Robinson's aerial power. Just like twelve months before, the stalemate could not be broken and the match needed extra time to separate the teams. In fact it was not until deep into the second period of extra time when, in the words of skipper Don Welsh, 'Centre forward Billy Robinson veered out to the right and crossed the ball hard. I went up and my head diverted it to the left. Before I could turn round I heard the ball whizz past me into the net.'

The scenes that followed are etched into the memories of all who were at Wembley that day. Chris Duffy, who had scored the goal, stood motionless after the ball entered the net until seeing the referee confirm the score by pointing to the centre circle. The little winger then took off and ran all the way down the pitch and into the arms of full-back Jack Shreeve, with other team members in hot pursuit. It remains one of the most joyous celebrations in Wembley history.

Shortly afterwards, Charlton's inspirational captain Don Welsh was followed up the famous steps to the Royal Box by his very good friend Sam Bartram and other team members, to receive the FA Cup from the Duke of Gloucester. The smiles on their faces then and after, as they paraded the cup for the supporters, still radiate from old photographs that record the Addicks' finest hour – or rather two hours.

Although Charlton played in white that afternoon, Sam certainly saw red on the way to the stadium. He recalled for the *People*, years later, 'That was a red-light journey if ever there was one. And I shall always look back on it with a smile. You know what the usual penalty is for crossing traffic lights at danger – a fine. Well, we crossed plenty that day. And we picked up a useful pre-match bonus' by doing so! This was how. We were given a police outrider, on a motorcycle, for the later stages of our journey to the stadium. At the first traffic lights we came to under

Charlton parade the FA Cup. Sam Bartram and Peter Croker carry captain Don Welsh around Wembley.

escort the red was showing against us. The cop waved to us to ignore it. One of our directors, Dr Montgomery, hadn't been looking. So when Don Welsh said, "Oh, we've just gone over against the red," the doctor began to get quite anxious. "We'll go past all the red lights today", the boys joked. "I bet we don't," said the doctor. We took him up on that. He agreed to pay £1 into a kitty every time we crossed against the red. And we were to give him the same for every 'green' crossing we made. What happened? We didn't come across one green light all the way! The red was showing all the time. And every time the police escort took us over it. The doc had to pay us about £10. "If your luck holds like this all day you'll win the cup," he grinned as we split the kitty between us. No need for me to tell you that our luck did hold. Chris Duffy's extra-time goal won us those precious gold medals that all of us cherish today.'

It was appropriate that winger Chris Duffy should be Charlton's cup final hero. He was the only player to appear in all league and cup matches that season and led the cup goal scorers. Teammates Bartram, Dawson, Hurst, Johnson, Phipps, Robinson and Shreeve were also ever-present in cup ties, while Bill Whittaker made his one and only FA Cup appearance in the final. Charlton Athletic became the thirty-third club win the FA Cup since its introduction in 1872, the only London professional teams to have previously lifted the trophy being Tottenham Hotspur and Arsenal.

At Wembley after the game, the players' families joined in the celebrations and there could have been none prouder than the Bartrams. Sam's mother and brothers Henry and Benny were on hand to get a close look at his winners' medal while young niece Marion was allowed what she recalls as 'a thimbleful of champagne from the FA Cup'.

There were many smiles on faces beyond Wembley and South East London that sunny April afternoon. Up in the North East there was also cause for celebration. At least seven of the players and officials on cup duty for Charlton were from that part of England. Sam and former Boldon Villa teammate, full-back Jack Shreeve, made up the Boldon Colliery connection; wing half Bert Johnson and inside right Tommy Dawson were signed from Durham club Spennymoor United; centre forward Bill Robinson was from Whitburn, near Sunderland, the home village of manager Jimmy Seed; Jimmy Trotter, the trainer, hailed from Newcastle.

So strong was the connection that on Charlton's first appearance in the region after their Wembley success they took the trophy with them for the match at Roker Park, Sunderland, in December. Following a 1-0 win, in which Robinson scored against his former club, the team made a stop at Boldon to parade the FA Cup. The Charlton coach pulled up outside the Co-op store near the colliery gates where a crowd had gathered. The team posed for photographs, then Sam and Jack Shreeve went home to spend the night nearby with their families while the others in the team moved on to their Newcastle hotel.

five

EUROPE, AUSTRALIA AND A RECORD

Addicks players and supporters were able to bask in FA Cup glory throughout the long summer of 1947. When the new Football League season began in late August, they ventured no further than The Valley for the first 2 matches. New signing Alex McCrae, an inside left from Hearts, contributed two goals in a 4-0 victory over Sheffield United on the opening day. The other changes from the Wembley line-up were fit-again Charlie Revell at left half and Benny Fenton at inside right. On the following Wednesday Arsenal drew an estimated 87,000 to Charlton and recorded a 4-2 win.

Sam, his fellow defenders and the fans must have wished they were still on holiday as six goals were leaked away to Manchester United on the Saturday and another half dozen at Highbury just four days later. There was some explanation for Arsenal's onslaught, as Charlton lost full-back Peter Croker through injury less than ten minutes into the game. Former Nunhead amateur centre forward Reg Lewis scored four of the Gunners' goals.

Things could only get better and fortunately they soon did. A 1-2 home defeat by Preston was followed by seven wins from the next 9 matches, with outstanding teamwork sometimes defying the odds. Addicks inside right Eric Lancelotte, who played in five of those victories, especially recalls the 1-0 success at Huddersfield. 'We all worked together with the backs and halves defending under constant pressure.' An own goal late in the game swung the result the Addicks' way.

When the long-awaited time came to start Charlton's FA Cup defence in January, they were rewarded with a home tie against Newcastle United, not that ground advantage had helped too much in the league that season, as already six First Division opponents had returned victorious from The Valley. A crowd of over 50,000 welcomed the cup holders and saw right winger Bill Robinson put the Addicks ahead after fifteen minutes. Visiting winger Tommy Pearson equalised for Newcastle before half-time. Then, early in the second half Charlie Revell, so unfortunate to miss both cup finals due to injury, restored Charlton's lead.

Newcastle's Pearson had a chance to score his second and level the scores but sent a penalty kick wide.

Charlton were safely into the fourth round and a fortnight later Stockport County were at The Valley. Revell was again on the scoresheet thanks to a first-half penalty. A Stockport own goal added to Charlton's tally before centre forward Charlie Vaughan completed a 3-0 win. The fifth round saw an away draw with Manchester United who, because of war damage to Old Trafford, were playing home matches on Manchester City's Maine Road ground. As City had also been drawn at home, United were obliged to play the tie at Huddersfield. This was a possible good omen for the Addicks, who had conceded six goals to United at Maine Road in August and fought spiritedly to overcome Huddersfield at Leeds Road more recently.

In the event Charlton fought a rearguard action but were outmanoeuvred by a United side that went on to win the cup for the second time in their history.

They were 2-0 winners over Charlton on the day, with goals in each half by Warner and Mitten. The fact that the second score did not come until minutes from time was due to an heroic goalkeeping performance by Bartram that saw him carried from the field by supporters after the final whistle. In the Manchester United team and soon to gain an FA Cup winners' medal was Charlton's wartime cup-winning centre half Allenby Chilton. Chilton, like Sam, was a product of Sunderland Schools' football.

Despite the cup setback, the team managed a mid-table finish to the First Division schedule and, for the first time in the club's Football League career, the Addicks recorded more wins on their travels than they did at The Valley. Bartram was the only ever-present member of a changing side.

In May Charlton made a brief trip to Ireland and won 2 of their 3 games, drawing the other, scoring 12 goals and conceding 6. Then, the summer of 1948 saw the Olympic Games in London with thirty-year-old Dutch housewife Fanny Blankers-Koen famously winning four gold medals on the cinder track

Despite a 0-2 defeat Sam is carried off the pitch by supporters at Hudderfield in 1948.

Attempting to keep hold of the cup! A determined Sam denies Manchester United's Jimmy Delaney and Jack Rowley in the fifth round at Huddersfield in 1948. United's 2-0 victory led to the cup moving from Charlton to Manchester.

at Wembley. Soccer was in the Olympic spotlight too as Europe claimed a clean sweep of medals with Sweden, Yugoslavia and Denmark taking gold, silver and bronze in an exclusively amateur competition.

The strength of continental football came as no surprise to Sam and his Charlton colleagues, who were no strangers to Europe. They followed up their 1946 close-season visit to Sweden with a series of testing one-off encounters on the continent. In September 1946 the Addicks suffered a 1-2 defeat in Portugal at the hands of Benfica and then on New Year's Day 1947 a visit to Paris resulted in a 2-2 draw with Stade Francais. This was followed in November 1947 with a 0-5 defeat by Liege in Belgium. In between times, old Swedish rivals Norrkoping visited Charlton and won an entertaining match 3-2. At centre forward for the

Charlton pose for the camera at Villa Park in October 1948. From left to right, back row: Jimmy Trotter (Trainer), Benny Fenton, Jack Shreeve, Sam Bartram, Alex McCrae, Frank Lock, Harold Phipps, Bill Whittaker. Front row: Gordon Hurst, Sid O'Linn, Charlie Vaughan, Charlie Revell, Tommy Brown, Chris Duffy.

Swedish club was Gunnar Nordahl, who later totalled 43 goals in 33 games for his country, including both goals in their 2-4 defeat by England at Highbury in November 1947 and seven in the 1948 Olympic Games. Like several of the successful Swedish Olympic team, he went on to play professionally in Italy, becoming AC Milan's all-time record scorer with 210 career goals.

After the 1948/49 campaign, which saw Charlton finish in the top half of the First Division, came an eventful tour to Istanbul in Turkey. Sixteen players made the four-game tour; Sam Bartram, Jimmy Campbell, Frank Lock, Jack Shreeve, Dudley Forbes, Malcolm Allison, Harold Phipps, Tommy Brown, Bert Johnson, Gordon Hurst, Charlie Purves, Dudley Davies, Charlie Vaughan, Riley Cullum, Chris Duffy and Jimmy D'Arcy. The opening match with Besiktas brought a 2-1 win and the following day the team recorded the same score against Galatasaray. The Addicks' performance dwindled in the second half of both matches but was rekindled for 3-0 and 5-0 wins over Fenerbahce and a Turkey Select XI the following week.

In the second match the English referee, accompanying the Charlton tour party, proved unpopular with the spectators, who threw stones at him and the players. Later Sam, remembering another game on the tour for the *Sunday People*, recalled, 'Apparently our opponents had temporarily lost their best two players, both on free transfers to the Turkish government as convicted wrongdoers! The club appealed for their release for a couple of hours to play against us. They were let out. One of them played outside left against Jimmy Campbell. This particular chunk of Turkish delight was a big fellow "inside" for stabbing a man to death. We were warned: "If he gets away from your back, Campbell, it's a certain goal." We passed the warning onto Jimmy. The game hadn't been going three minutes

Referee Bert Griffiths watches as captain Bartram greets Saarbrucken skipper Clemens on Charlton's visit in May 1949.

when the big fellow broke through. Jimmy, instead of shadowing him, stood stock still in his path. The convict crashed into him, toppled head first over Jimmy's shoulder and knocked himself out on the iron-hard pitch. He was immediately taken off on a stretcher, back to the Turkish equivalent of Pentonville. His mate lasted the game out – then went back under escort to his cell.'

Also in May 1949, Charlton played a match in Allied-occupied Germany when they met Saarbrucken. The Addicks were a major attraction as they were the first English team to visit the area for thirty-seven years. Sam was captain for the day and much to his surprise received a bouquet of flowers and a kiss on both cheeks from a German girl when the teams lined-up before the kick-off.

Top British referee Bert Griffiths was invited to take charge of the game and he recalled, 'I arrived before the Charlton team and had a chance to assess the feeling of the local people. Excitement was terrific. When the kick-off time came the ground was packed and many more spectators sat on the arms of the telegraph poles that towered outside the ground. One feature of the game, which I will never forget, was a grand series of saves made by Sam Bartram, who played so brilliantly that the crowd eventually came on to the field to congratulate him.' Charlton won the match 1–0.

Despite the successes in Turkey and Germany, when the new season began at home things proved less fortunate, with six defeats and just 3 wins in the first 10 games. There was an early highlight when inside forward Tommy Lumley, signed from northern club Consett, scored a hat-trick in the 6–3 home win over Newcastle

The line-up for the match shown in the programme.

United in September. Later that month goalkeeper Sam visited the North-East for a special fixture at Roker Park, Sunderland, where he lined up in an Ex-North-East League XI against a combined Sunderland and Middlesbrough team.

Playing with Sam was Charlie Purvis, who Charlton signed from Spennymoor United in 1947. The match was a fundraiser for the league's new offices, their Sunderland headquarters having been demolished by enemy action during the Second World War. The teams were: Ex-North-East League XI: Bartram (Charlton Athletic); Milburn (Chesterfield), Howe (Derby County); Johnson (Grimsby Town), Chilton (Manchester United), McGlen (Manchester United); Hudson Chesterfield), Hagan (Sheffield United), Juliussen (Consett), Purves (Charlton Athletic), Fenton (Blackburn Rovers). Sunderland/Middlesbrough: Ugolini; Robinson, Hardwick (all Middlesbrough); Scotson, Walsh, Watson (all Sunderland); Spuhler (Middlesbrough), Kirtley, Broadis, Shackleton (all Sunderland), Hartnett (Middlesbrough).

In addition to providing a springboard to league football for many players, Huddersfield Town, Bradford Park Avenue, Hartlepools United, Darlington and South Shields had also graduated to Football League status after playing in the North-East League. Plenty of post-war household names in the match line-up but perhaps not so well known south of the border was the Ex-North East League XI centre forward Albert Juliussen, Consett's player/manager. Juliussen was born in Northumberland and played for Cramlington Black Watch and Huddersfield Town before becoming a Dundee favourite with 95 goals from 73 games in the

Sam and Harold Phipps (right) in action against Middlesbrough, with Boro's Wilf Mannion (centre) looking on.

1940s. These included 13 in consecutive outings in 1947 – six against Alloa and seven against Dunfermline.

As for the game, 20,151 spectators raised £1,800 for the North East League. The *Northern Echo* reported that Sam was 'his usual brilliant self'.

Other than the victory over Newcastle it was not a good season for Charlton against North-East opponents. However, they did achieve a notable victory over arch rivals Arsenal at Highbury for the first time. The 3-2 win in November

Sam wins an aerial duel with Bolton Wanderers' centre forward Nat Lofthouse during a 0-0 draw at The Valley in November 1949.

marked Derek Ufton's second appearance for the club. Wingers Billy Kiernan and Gordon Hurst, plus centre forward Charlie Vaughan, were the scorers. Despite fluctuating league form, the home FA Cup third round tie with Fulham attracted a crowd of over 50,000, who saw a 2-2 draw. Gordon Hurst twice put the Addicks ahead, only for Fulham to equalise. In the replay a goal in each half from inside forward Jimmy D'Arcy and Charlie Vaughan eased Charlton through 2-1.

Home advantage again failed to prove decisive in the fourth round when Cardiff City drew 1-1 at The Valley, then extended the team's woes by winning the replay 2-0. Only 5 further wins followed that season, two of them in the final 2 games of the campaign. Back-to-back 2-0 and 2-1 victories over Birmingham City at The Valley and Derby County at the Baseball Ground were just sufficient to place Charlton third from bottom, the lowest finish in the club's First Division history.

Nevertheless, two reader's letters to the *News Chronicle* put Sam on top of the tree. Douglas Cole from Amersham claimed, 'Sam Bartram, now in his sixteenth season at The Valley, is still the best 'keeper in the UK and if there were any justice in the football world he would also be in his sixteenth season for England.' Mr A.G. Smith of Plumstead stressed, 'Charlton are fortunate in the possession of two priceless assets. In Jimmy Seed they have one of the shrewdest and most far-sighted managers in football, and in Sam Bartram a goalkeeper whom everyone excepting apparently the England selectors recognises as of international class.'

The following season started with a shock when Bolton Wanderers visited The Valley and took the lead with the new season just eight seconds old. The scorer was Wanderers' centre forward Nat Lofthouse, who went on to complete a hat-trick. He also won the first of his many England caps shortly afterwards. Not to be outdone on this occasion, Charlton outscored Bolton to win 4-3. They followed up with a 3-1 victory over Fulham at Craven Cottage, then a visit to Blackpool.

The *Sunday Pictorial* reporter, who joined the resort's summer holiday-makers at the match, waxed lyrical about the game. 'The hallmark of this magnificent goal-less game, which Blackpool ought to have won, was the sportsmanship of both sides, accompanied by handshakes all round and back-slapping between veteran Sam Bartram and ebullient Stanley Mortenson. Charlton would have fallen but for the composure and steadiness of their first-class defence and Bartram's superb goalkeeping.'

A week later newly promoted Tottenham Hotspur drew a crowd of 61,480 to The Valley. Alf Ramsey, England's World Cup-winning manager in 1966, opened the scoring with a first-half penalty for Spurs, in a 1-1 draw.

In October, cup holders Arsenal attracted a gate of 63,539 and emerged 3-1 winners, but it was the return 'derby' at Highbury in February 1951 that made history. In mid-season Charlton had acquired the services of Swedish amateur centre forward Hans Jeppson, who was on a three-month business studies trip to London. He wrote his name into Addicks folklore by scoring 9 goals in 11 games, three of them in the 5-2 away victory over Arsenal. It was the first time in their fifty-eight-year Football League career that a visiting London club had put that many goals past the Gunners, either at Plumstead or Highbury.

Jeppson's exploits not only hit the headlines but also had the effect of saving Charlton in a difficult season. The club won 7 and drew 2 of the games in which he played and the points gained were sufficient to keep them in the First Division. Following the home game with Portsmouth in March, with just 5 matches remaining in the season, he was rushed down the Thames by motor boat to Tilbury to catch the evening boat home to Sweden and disappeared into the sunset.

Well, not quite. The blond-haired Swedish international had attracted so much attention during his brief spell at Charlton that shortly afterwards he was offered a highly paid contract in Italy, where he played successfully for Atalanta and Napoli.

The summer of 1951 saw goalkeeper Bartram heading even further afield. Sam was selected for the Football Association party to visit Australia on a twenty-one match tour over three months. Joining him were Charlton colleagues winger Gordon Hurst and full-back Frank Lock. The full touring team was: Goalkeepers: Sam Bartram (Charlton Athletic), Ted Burgin (Sheffield United); Backs: Harry Bamford (Bristol Rovers), John McCue (Stoke City), Frank Lock (Charlton Athletic); Half-Backs: Derek Parker (West Ham United), Reg Flewin (Portsmouth,

THE NOVELETTES VARIETY PRODUCTIONS
present

Personal Appearances of

SAM   PETER   HAROLD   GORDON
BARTRAM • CROKER • PHIPPS • HURST

STARS OF CHARLTON ATHLETIC F.C.

LEWISHAM ACCORDION CLUB BAND
Directed by LEN STILES

AND A FIRST-CLASS VARIETY BILL, including
" THE SINGING WAITERS "
Five Artists from RALPH READER'S FAMOUS GANG 'SHOW'

in
VARIETY VENTURE
(Produced by DEREK ALLEN)

IN AID OF
The BRITISH EMPIRE CANCER CAMPAIGN
Under the patronage of
His Worship THE MAYOR & THE MAYORESS
OF LEWISHAM

THURS. MARCH 22nd, 1951 at 7.45

TICKETS :   5/- : 3/6 : 2/6 & 1/6
Special reduced rates to recognised Clubs, etc. from :
14 Lee Park, S.E.3.   56 Geraint Road,   or Town Hall Booking Office

An advertisement for a stage appearance of Charlton players in a variety show, 1951.

Captain), Syd Owen (Luton Town), Joe Shaw (Sheffield United), Leo Kieran (Tranmere Rovers); Forwards: Frank Broome (Notts County), Harry Webster (Bolton Wanderers), Bill Smith (Birmingham City), Ike Clarke (Portsmouth), Jackie Sewell (Sheffield Wednesday), Jimmy Hagan (Sheffield United), Bobby Langton (Bolton Wanderers), Gordon Hurst (Charlton Athletic); Trainer: Bob Shotton (Barnsley); FA members-in-charge: David Wiseman and Frank Adams.

Currency regulations meant players were not permitted to take more than £5 out of the country but they were paid an allowance of £1 10s per day during the tour. No bonuses were paid in respect of the tour matches.

Australian magazine *Sporting Life* carried an article in their April edition with the heading 'SAM'LL GIVE US A LESSON IN SOCCER. Sam Bartram will teach us a few things when he arrives with the English soccer team. He's one of the greatest goalies.' It began, 'Australia may be Cock of the Walk at cricket, but England is likely to hand her a few lessons in Soccer this season. The touring English team will be one of the strongest ever sent abroad with some of the most brilliant individual players of the decade. Of the outstanding group, none is more spectacular than auburn-haired dare-devil goalkeeper Sam Bartram. In a dozen countries his spectacular dives and spring-heeled leaps have been decisive factors in big matches. Bartram, a burly, thirty-seven-year-old six-footer, with intense blue eyes, an attractive wife and a five-year-old daughter, attracts a fan-mail – mostly from teenaged girls – unequalled by any English soccer star. Each season he spends two nights a week and a small fortune answering it.'

FA team to Australia 1951. From left to right, back row: R. Langton (Bolton Wanderers),
F. Broome (Notts County), E. Burgin (Sheffield United), I. Clarke (Portsmouth), H. Webster
(Bolton Wanderers), D. Parker (West Ham United). Middle row: R. Shotton (Trainer),
L. Kieran (Tranmere Rovers), W. Smith (Birmingham City), H. Bamford (Bristol Rovers),
S. Bartram (Charlton Athletic), J. McCue (Stoke City), J. Shaw (Sheffield United). Front
row: G. Hurst (Charlton Athletic), J. Sewell (Sheffield Wednesday), R. Flewin (Portsmouth,
Captain), D. Wiseman (FA), F. Adams (FA), S. Owen (Luton Town), F. Lock (Charlton
Athletic), J. Hagan (Sheffield United).

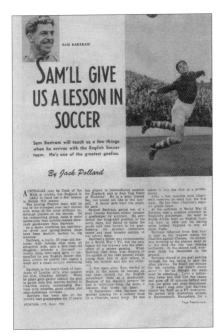

From Australian magazine *Sporting Life*,
April 1951.

Just two days after the end of the season the FA party assembled at the Great Western Hotel Paddington, moved on to Australia House in The Strand for a reception given by the Acting High Commissioner for Australia, then took the night flight to New York. After sightseeing in the city, a match was played against American League All Stars, which was won 4-0. Then it was off to San Francisco, where lunch was provided by San Francisco FC, and onward to Australia, with refuelling stops at Honolulu, Canton Island and Fiji. The overall trip to Sydney took five days.

The tour opened with a 7-0 win over South Coast at Wollongong and an 8-1 victory against New South Wales. At the latter game on the Sydney Showground, according to Australia's *Soccer Weekly News*, 'The 42,150 attendance was treated to the greatest display of Association Football ever seen in Australia. The Englishmen scented mastery early, and revelled in pattern-weaving movements, elaborate as they were speedy and spell-binding.' Following a 6-2 success in game three against Metropolis, also in Sydney, the eagerly awaited first international of the tour took place on Saturday 26 May. The teams for the game on the Sydney Cricket Ground were: Australia: Norman Conquest; Kevin O'Neill, Cec Drummond; Bob Lawrie (Captain), Tom Jack, Eric Duff; Dick Kemp, George Russell, Frank Parsons, Malcolm Wild, Harry Robertson. England XI: Sam Bartram; Harry Bamford, Frank Lock; Joe Shaw, Reg Flewin (Captain), Leo Kieran; Gordon Hurst, Jackie Sewell, Ike Clarke, Jimmy Hagan, Bobby Langton. The attendance at the match, won 4-1 by England, was 46,104. The scorers were Jackie Sewell (2), Ike Clarke and Gordon Hurst.

Then followed a leg of the journey that must have seemed like 'home from home' for Sam. The party travelled to Newcastle, New South Wales, for 2 matches. The first was in the mining town of Cessnock, where the majority of the workforce were settlers from Britain who were well versed in English soccer. Here the players received a great reception before and after their 7-1 victory over the Combined Northern Districts. The second match in Newcastle, with New South Wales, produced the closest match of the tour so far, when the England XI won 3-1 in a robust affair on a hard surface.

The next 3 games were in Melbourne, where Jackie Sewell scored all seven goals in one of two wins over Victoria. The other was a 6-1 victory over an Australian XI. The party then moved on to Tasmania and recorded two wins, 11-0 and 17-0. In the latter Jimmy Hagan netted eight goals. The next match at Adelaide against an Australian XI was also a high-scoring affair. Ike Clarke and Jimmy Hagan both scored four times in the 13-1 win. Ted Burgin was in goal that day but, in his autobiography, Sam recalls a special visitor to the England XI dressing room. 'After the game a small man with a deeply tanned face and a friendly smile joined us in the dressing room. "Well done, boys," he said, shaking hands with several members of the team. "You played splendidly. I shouldn't really enjoy seeing an Australian team lose, but I must say that I found every minute of the game entertaining." It was the most famous of all Australians, the great cricketer Sir Donald Bradman.'

Charlton colleagues on the FA tour to Australia, Sam Bartram, Gordon Hurst and Frank Lock.

Heavy rain in Sydney caused the cancellation of a scheduled pre-Test match fixture and resulted in the pitch for the second international of the series, at the Sydney Cricket Ground, resembling a quagmire. The conditions suited the English players better than their opponents, so much so that the England XI won 17-0. The teams were: Australia: Norman Conquest; Hedley Parkes, Cec Drummond; Bob Lawrie (Captain), Tom Jack, Eric Duff; Dick Kemp, Eric Hulme, Reg Date, Malcolm Wild, Ross McKenzie. England XI: Sam Bartram; Harry Bamford, John McCue; Derek Parker, Reg Flewin (Captain), Joe Shaw; Gordon Hurst, Jackie Sewell, Ike Clarke, Jimmy Hagan, Frank Broome. The England XI scorers were Sewell (6), Clarke (4), Hagan (3), Broome (3) and Hurst. Three of Clarke's goals were scored in a four-minute period.

Next it was north to Queensland for a three-match stopover in Brisbane. Queensland were beaten 7-1 prior to the Third Test on the Brisbane Cricket Ground, which ended 4-1 to the England XI, with a crowd of 23,216 seeing two goals from Clarke and one each by Hagan and Langton. The line-ups were: Australia: Ron Lord; Kevin O'Neill, Cec Drummond; Bob Lawrie (Captain), Bob Bignall, Eric Duff; Jock Hodge, Eric Hulme, Gordon Nunn, Jock McMahon, Harry Robertson. England XI: Sam Bartram; Harry Bamford, John McCue; Reg Flewin (Captain), Joe Shaw, Derek Parker; Gordon Hurst, Jackie Sewell, Jimmy Hagan, Bobby Langton, Ike Clarke.

The FA party in Australia.

In the third game in the region, an hour's flight from Brisbane at Bundaberg, a home player fractured a leg but bravely played on as the visitors romped home 13-1. After twelve sunny days in Queensland it was back to Sydney for the fourth international of the series at the Sydney Showground. An alternative sporting attraction, a rugby league fixture between New South Wales and France, took place on the adjoining Sydney Cricket Ground and affected the gate, which was a pity because

Australia played their best soccer of the summer, which made for an excellent contest. Harry Webster scored a hat-trick as the England XI won 6-1. The teams for the Fourth Test were: Australia: Ron Lord; Kevin O'Neill, Cec Drummond; Bob Lawrie (Captain), Bob Bignall, Eric Duff; Kevin Lake, Eric Hulme, Frank Parsons, Jock McMahon, Harry Robertson. England XI: Sam Bartram; Harry Bamford, John McCue; Frank Lock, Syd Owen (Captain), Joe Shaw; Gordon Hurst, Frank Broome (Harry Webster), Jackie Sewell, Ike Clarke, Bobby Langton. The match programme gave details of a function in honour of the FA team two days later where there would be, 'a fashion parade by twenty-four mannequins of Miss June Dally-Watkins's studio. The lovely young ladies will parade in Australian sports clothes and demonstrate the famous Darling Folding Umbrellas.'

The Test match was followed with a game versus Granville District at Parramatta, which was well fought by the home team and the England XI only pulled clear in the second-half, winning 5-2. Then it was back to Newcastle for the final Test match on the Newcastle Showground. A strong, cold wind affected the conditions and restricted the crowd to 14,000. The teams were: Australia: Ron Lord; Bob Bignall, Kevin O'Neill; Bob Lawrie (Captain), Tom Jack, Lex Gibb; Sid North, Eric Hulme, Gordon Nunn, Alec Heaney, Harry Robertson. England XI: Ted Burgin; Harry Bamford, John McCue; Derek Parker, Reg Flewin (Captain), Joe Shaw; Gordon Hurst, Jackie Sewell, Ike Clarke, Bill Smith, Bobby Langton. The England XI won 5-0, with Clarke (2), Sewell, Smith and Hurst the scorers.

The final game of the tour was at Wollongong against South Coast and by now injuries were restricting selection, with full-back John McCue and Sam the only fully fit team members. Nevertheless, a team was scraped together and the FA party edged home 2-0. In total 21 matches were played, all of which were won. Jackie Sewell topped the goal scorers with 35, followed by Jimmy Hagan on 28 and Ike Clarke with 23. Charlton right winger Gordon Hurst, who played in all 5 Test matches, claimed 12.

On the journey home the team enjoyed a six-hour stopover at Honolulu, where they were greeted and entertained by the Hawaiian Society, who presented garlands to every member of the party and took them on an island tour. It was then on to San Francisco, Boston, Shannon and Heathrow. Having started out on 7 May, the party returned home on 28 July. The distance covered on the tour was a staggering 31,000 miles and the team was airborne for a total of 126 hours.

The official FA report concludes, 'The tour was undoubtedly a very successful one, as we gave to the Australians something in football that they had never before experienced. One can say that the play of our team completely fascinated the Australians and it was soon evident that our ability and sportsmanship completely captivated them. Tremendous interest was taken throughout Australia and tributes to the skill of our players were paid throughout the country. It was evident that the Australian players were keen to learn and in many of the later games one could see them using some of the tactics exploited by our players.'

Little could the Australian Soccer Football Association, who then administered a totally amateur game, have anticipated that, half a century later, a team of mostly English-based Australian professionals would upset England in a full international match on British soil. The 'Socceroos' won 3-1 at Upton Park, West Ham in 2003.

Three weeks after returning home from Australia, Sam was in action for Charlton in the opening fixture of the 1951/52 season. Burnley were beaten at The Valley by the only goal of the game and, after a 0-3 midweek defeat at Preston, a run of eight close results followed, including three wins and three draws. During this spell South African defender John Hewie made his debut at Fratton Park, Portsmouth. 'Long John' had been a spectator at Durban in 1939 when Sam played there for the English tourists. He became a great servant of Charlton and one of the finest footballers to wear their colours. No one would have predicted it then but, later in his career, he was selected to keep goal in 4 Football League matches.

The Addicks were having a much better season and scored three or more goals for the fourth time in the first 11 games when they beat cup holders Newcastle 3-0. Subsequently, Sam saved from the penalty spot in successive home games to maintain an impressive Valley record. First he saved against Sunderland, when he foiled Len Shackleton. A fortnight later he spoilt Huddersfield Town winger Vic Metcalfe's 100 per cent penalty success record. A third penalty save at The Valley in March, from Allan Brown's spot kick, enabled Charlton to complete the double over Blackpool.

The following match against Arsenal at Highbury saw Sam reach a career milestone when he broke Norman Smith's Charlton record of 417 League appearances. Appropriately, the long-serving full-back, who was also a native of the North-East, had been in the team when Bartram made his debut in 1934 and had played alongside Sam in all his early outings for the club. Coincidentally, Smith was signed from Usworth Colliery, County Durham, close to the Bartram family home at Boldon, in 1922 and figured in both Charlton's Third Division championship-winning seasons of 1928/29 and 1934/35.

Although the game at Highbury resulted in a 2-1 victory for Arsenal, Bartram managed eleven clean sheets over the season and Charlton finished in the top half of the First Division for the first time in three years.

By now Sam Bartram & Co. Ltd, the sports outfitters business, in Floyd Road near The Valley, was well established. The thousands of spectators approaching the ground from the direction of Charlton Station could not fail to notice his sports shop in its prominent position on the corner of Floyd Road and Valley Grove. For years it was a landmark for fans on their route to and from The Valley. To young supporters it was an Aladdin's cave, the forerunner of today's football club shops, not just selling boots, footballs, studs and laces but, most excitingly, postcard-size portraits of Charlton players and other famous footballers.

Above and overleaf: Shopkeeper Sam.

Naturally passers-by would look in, hoping for a glimpse of Sam, but would be lucky to see him unless they arrived well before kick-off. On match days Sam's wife Helen ran the shop and closed up before the game so she could watch the match. At other times, any youngsters who did find Sam on duty in the shop were made very welcome but were often too nervous and tongue-tied to talk at length with their hero.

Hero he certainly was and not just with the supporters. Sam constantly caught the attention of the media. Midway through the 1951/52 season John Arlott, that king of sports writers and commentators, wrote in the *Evening News*, 'In the Kentish corner of London "Sam" is enough to identify Charlton's red-haired goalkeeper. Over seventeen years with the club – he came from Boldon Colliery, near manager Jimmy Seed's home, in 1934 – ought to make him a veteran. But nobody who has watched him could honestly give him such a label. A man is as old as he feels, and Sam Bartram, on his great days, feels too young to be pegged to the ground. Cast

Benny Fenton (centre left) and Jack Shreeve lead a brisk pre-training walk past Sam's shop.

an eye in his direction sometimes when he is not in action. With the ball forty yards away you will see Sam on tiptoe, arms lifted and gloved hands palms downward, looking somewhat like Toscanini about to call the NBC orchestra into action. When the play moves to his goal he is revealed as a great but human goalkeeper. Some of the great masters – like Hibbs or Sam Hardy – have been almost inhumanly perfect, moving coldly into position to catch the ball with as cold an efficiency. Sam Bartram makes mistakes; but he has a gloriously human way of retrieving them. He can start to move the wrong way and still get back to make a save. But he is even more than a goalkeeper. Anyone who saw Charlton take two points from Spurs at White Hart Lane will remember the day when Sam was half the game. Charlton defended heroically, but Bartram rolled human miracles off the arm – catching, punching, diving with a supremely judged recklessness at the feet of advancing forwards, kicking a prodigious length. And he stood, in his rare easy moments of that second half, as a mud-spattered and slightly battered man who was enjoying himself to the utmost. Wartime caps and two overseas tours are all the tangible honours the game has given Sam Bartram, but he has left a clearer mark than many internationals on those who have watched him, for with Stanley Matthews and Tommy Harmer he is the best afternoon's worth of entertainment in modern football.'

Early next season the *Daily Express* report of a 1–1 draw at Portsmouth carried the following headline, 'Sam Bartram Silences the Pompey Barrage,' under which Desmond Hackett wrote, 'Mighty Sam Bartram, that teak-hard gallant among goalkeepers, growled his satisfaction after this all-excitement soccer piece at

Portsmouth last night. Bartram had a running commentary duel with the crowd, a personal battle with Portsmouth centre forward Albert Mundy, and in between blasted high-powered criticism at his own defence when he thought their tackling was too timid. What a man is this Bartram. However he recovered from the first ten minutes of Portsmouth's barrage plan we shall never know. The Charlton goal had become a shooting range with the shots cracking from Gaillard, Gordon, Dickinson, Phillips, Gaillard again and another Phillips threat. Finally Bartram fell over backwards and young Gordon shot over that empty much-abused goal.'

The *Daily Mail* headline for the same game read, 'Bartram Was Really Great.' Their report opened, 'Charlton Athletic had goalkeeper Sam Bartram to thank that they were not overwhelmed by a much-improved Portsmouth side at Fratton Park. From the hectic opening minutes, when he saved a succession of on-the-target shots from the lively home forwards, to the thrilling climax of a fast, entertaining game, he was never at fault. His brilliant anticipation prevented at least three goals. Early on he turned a flashing thirty-yard drive from Dickinson round the post for a corner. Just before half-time he clutched a back-header by his teammate Campbell from under the bar. And, to round off a grand display, he miraculously punched a shrewd Mundy lob safely over the bar when 25,000 spectators were all ready to shout "goal."'

After Charlton's 2-1 win at Bolton, Sam hit the national headlines again. The *Daily Mirror* led with, 'Star turn by the man with "elastic" arms. Sam Bartram, Charlton goalkeeper, is wasted on the football field. He ought to go on the halls, billed as "The Man with the elastic arms." He went through his repertoire at Bolton yesterday – and Charlton won 2-1 largely because he never missed a trick. In the first and last minutes, Bartram made "impossible" fingertip saves from headers by Moir, Scottish international inside right, who captained Bolton in the absence of right-back Jack Ball.'

Another national newspaper said, 'The astonishing thirty-eight-year-old Sam, nineteen years with Charlton ("I always say I'm twenty-one, because in football over twenty-one you're a veteran") practically played Nat Lofthouse and co. on his own after Charlton, midway through the second half, had snatched a 2-1 lead. It may be that a brilliant early save by Bartram from Moir inspired Charlton… then came the Bolton barrage, which Sam – aided by a little of the luck all goalkeepers must have – repelled. Hewie, switched to left-back because Lock is injured, gave a polished show and centre half Ufton prevented Lofthouse from worrying Bartram too much.'

Coincidentally, earlier that season, Charlton's Derek Ufton and Bolton's Nat Lofthouse played together in the England team that drew 4-4 with the Rest of the World at Wembley. At centre forward for the visitors that afternoon was Sweden's Gunnar Nordahl, who played for Norrkoping in a friendly match at The Valley in 1946. Ufton, a good friend of Sam, became the first Charlton player to win a full England cap since Don Welsh in 1939.

Sam in training at the valley.

A 1-0 win over Chelsea at Stamford Bridge was introduced thus, 'Sam Bartram Stole Show. Heaven preserve me from any more so-called "local derbies" this season. I haven't yet seen one which produced good football. Viewing this game in retrospect I can only see a maze of red and blue jerseys, running around and getting in each other's way, with every now and again a brilliant green one floating above them and picking the ball out of the skies. That I recognise from the coppery head which surmounts it, as the jersey of one Sam Bartram, of sure judgement, whose goalkeeping time and again has saved Charlton and brought home the points to The Valley.'

The *News Chronicle*, reporting the 0-1 defeat at Stoke, led with headline, 'Bartram again stands alone' and continued, 'It was those two men again – Stoke's centre forward Roy Brown and Charlton's Sam Bartram. They were the showpieces of this untidy game. Apart from his goal, an eighteenth-minute header and worth a small fortune to the safety-bidding City – Brown was the life and soul of his side. He was everywhere, worrying Charlton's faltering defence into mistakes and piling up chances that should have meant goals. But Bartram, chief stumbling block to a big Stoke win, only just lost the battle. His best spell was in the last three blistering minutes when the goal-hungry Stoke forwards nipped in four great drives – and Bartram made four great saves.'

The *Sunday Dispatch*, covering Burnley's 2-0 win over Charlton at Turf Moor began, 'Sam Bartram almost robbed Burnley of two points. In the first half he made some splendid interceptions, cutting out centres and holding everything that came his way. Then he got the cheers with a remarkable save from Stephenson when the young winger was right through. It was unlucky for Bartram that the men in front of him were not as safe. Defensive slips were responsible for the two goals by Holden and Shannon.'

Charlton were well placed in the league and the *Star* newspaper was optimistic about their title chances. 'Sam Bartram, Charlton's long-serving goalkeeper, is within sight of a trio of soccer trophies, which have been collected by only five other players in modern soccer. If Charlton finish top of the First Division, Bartram will add a league championship medal to a FA Cup winners' medal and a cup runners-up medal. The only present-day players to achieve this rare distinction are all from Arsenal – George Swindin, Joe Mercer, Laurie Scott, Wally Barnes and Jimmy Logie. They took part in the 1950 and 1952 finals and helped Arsenal to win the League in 1947/48... He was unlucky not to gain a full cap for England. His peak years coincided with the war and the ascendancy of Frank Swift immediately afterwards. In this respect Bartram is like Swindin; the other four Arsenal players have all been capped. Now thirty-nine, Bartram has no immediate thought of retiring. He tells me he would like to go on playing until 1955, when his twenty-first anniversary at The Valley would coincide with the club's fiftieth birthday.'

At the start of April the Addicks occupied second place in the table but the defeats at Stoke and Burnley and other late season setbacks restricted their challenge. Despite winning the final fixture at home to Spurs 3-2, they had to settle for fifth place, five points behind Arsenal, who won the championship on goal average from Preston North End. One of their best results was a 4-3 win at Highbury in September, over the eventual champions, in front of a 60,000 crowd.

Trainer Jimmy Trotter puts Cyril Hammond, Sam Bartram, John Hewie, Benny Fenton and Derek Ufton through their paces.

When Arsenal visited The Valley in January, Sam made his 450th Football League appearance. He was made captain for the day and a massive attendance of 66,555 saw Gordon Hurst score both goals in a 2-2 draw. A few weeks later, after a 0-0 home draw with Newcastle, the *Sunday Pictorial* carried a feature entitled, 'SAY THANKS TO SAM WITH HOLIDAY TOUR,' in which Scottie Hall said, 'Holidays are rewards for application and dedication to the job, aren't they? I know a certain Mister Samuel Bartram who's worked for a whopping good holiday, and I've just thought of a very good time and place for it. Sam Bartram, Charlton goalkeeper for nineteen glorious years, the greatest of football's great uncapped, should be asked to join the FA in their business/pleasure South American summer tour. Here would be a long overdue official thank you to a great goal-keeper and a great character and an entertainer in his own right whom England's soccer crowds have now been thanking with warm applause on some 460 soccer afternoons… The FA took him to South Africa in 1939, Australia in 1951. That to me was just a "whispered" official thank you. The FA failed and neglected Bartram by not taking him to Wembley or Hampden for a "full" international. Since, checking on his age, thirty-nine, they are now unlikely to give Bartram the cap he should have had ten or more years ago, they really must say "sorry" with this South American trip.' Of Sam's contribution in the 0-0 draw, he added, 'This then was yet another occasion when Bartram, crisp and colourful, came to the rescue of a game that was very wobbly at the knees. Why, even in the second half,

The victorious London team in Genoa, June 1953. From left to right, back row: Referee, W. Nicholson (Tottenham Hotspur), D. Roper (Arsenal), S. Bartram (Charlton Athletic), D. Lishman (Arsenal), E. Lowe (Fulham), B. Jezzard (Fulham). Front row: J. Logie (Arsenal), S. Willemse (Chelsea), F. Monk (Brentford), G. Hurst (Charlton Athletic), W. Dickson (Chelsea).

when Newcastle's numbed nervousness rendered him almost jobless, you saw the man's quality. You saw the big, banjo eyes roaming the field. Everywhere the ball went the big, banjo eyes went with it. Watching somebody else hard at work, just for a change, was one of the great workers of 'em all.'

Four days after the draw with Newcastle, Sam was London's skipper in a game with Berlin at Highbury. The teams that evening were: London: Sam Bartram (Charlton Athletic); Freddie Monk (Brentford), Stan Willemse (Chelsea); Ken Armstrong (Chelsea), Gerry Bowler (Millwall), Bill Dickson (Chelsea); Billy Gray (Chelsea), Jimmy Logie (Arsenal), Cliff Holton (Arsenal), Charlie Vaughan (Charlton Athletic), Billy Kiernan (Charlton Athletic). Berlin: O. Schadebordt (BSV 92); A. Gaulke (Viktotia 89), R. Strehlow (Union 06); H. Jonas (Viktoria 89), H. Brand (Viktoria 89), E. Wittig (Tennis Borussia); E. Wax (Union 06), G. Graf (Tennis Borussia), H. Ritter (Spandauer Sportverein), W. Herter (Viktoria 89), H. Schultz (Union 06). Berlin were the first German representative team to play in Britain since the war. London won the match, which was shown on BBC television, 6–1. Charlton's Billy Kiernan and Charlie Vaughan each scored twice. London's other two goals were scored by Arsenal centre forward Cliff Holton, who became a Charlton player twelve years later.

On 4 June Sam lined-up in London's next fixture, away to Genoa at the Luigi Ferraris Stadium. The full London team, winners by 2–1 was; Sam Bartram (Charlton Athletic); Freddie Monk (Brentford), Stan Willemse (Chelsea); Bill Nicholson (Tottenham Hotspur, Captain), Bill Dickson (Chelsea), Eddie Lowe

Sam in the foreground at the official dinner after London *v.* Berlin, March 1953.

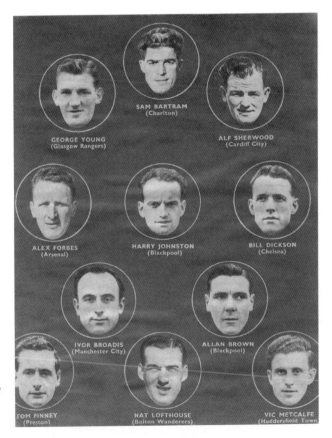

Charles Buchan's Football Monthly Team of the Year 1953.

(Fulham); Gordon Hurst (Charlton Athletic), Jimmy Logie (Arsenal), Bedford Jezzard (Fulham), Doug Lishman (Arsenal), Don Roper (Arsenal).

In the summer the leading soccer magazine, *Charles Buchan's Football Monthly*, published their team of players of the year. Charles Buchan's personal selections were: Goalkeeper: Sam Bartram (Charlton Athletic,); Right-Back: George Young (Glasgow Rangers); Left-Back: Alf Sherwood (Cardiff City); Right Half: Alex Forbes (Arsenal); Centre Half: Harry Johnston (Blackpool); Left Half: Bill Dickson (Chelsea); Outside Right: Tom Finney (Preston North End); Inside Right: Ivor Broadis (Manchester City); Centre Forward: Nat Lofthouse (Bolton Wanderers); Inside Left: Allan Brown (Blackpool); Outside Left: Vic Metcalfe (Huddersfield Town).

six

GOALKEEPING IN THE GRAND MANNER

The 1953/54 Charlton Athletic handbook carried the following paragraph: 'This story would not be complete without a special reference to Sam Bartram, Charlton's evergreen goalkeeper and president of the Robins Club. By the end of last season Sam had made 467 league appearances with Charlton – more than any other goalkeeper in the country, and his legion of friends are hoping he will have the luck to continue in harness to complete, in 1955, his twenty-first year with Charlton. A grand goalkeeper and a grand fellow.'

When the season began, for the second year in succession Charlton's first opponents were Sunderland. Almost 50,000 were at The Valley to see a 5-3 victory. A 3-1 home win over Burnley four days later completed a promising start to the new campaign. Unfortunately 4 defeats in the next 5 games slowed the Addicks' progress but things soon improved. In September Middlesbrough were beaten 8-1 at The Valley and a fortnight later Liverpool were outplayed to the tune of 6-0.

A 2-0 success at Newcastle in October produced the following headline in the *News of the World*, 'BARTRAM STOPS EVERYTHING.' The match report added, 'Newcastle threw all they knew into a second-half rally. Defence didn't seem to matter. It took them ten minutes of break-neck effort to get in the first shot. After that it was Bartram *v.* Newcastle United. Shots from Keery, Casey, Mitchell, Milburn and Scouler rained in on the veteran Sam. He was beaten only once by Mitchell, but Ellis was there to clear. Milburn played all over the line and he had bad luck in having a Sam Bartram to beat. Goalkeeping less brilliant than the veteran Sam's must have resulted in a crushing defeat for Charlton.'

The victory ensured maximum interest in Charlton's next home game. The visitors were popular cup-winners Blackpool and 56,664 witnessed a 4-2 Charlton win. Two weeks later an even bigger crowd, 60,259, saw the 'derby' with Arsenal, which ended 5-1 in favour of the Gunners. In between, the Addicks' run of 6 consecutive wins that amassed 25 goals came to an end with a 1-3 defeat at Portsmouth, where, according to the *Sunday Dispatch*, 'BARTRAM DESERVED

ALL THE APPLAUSE.' 'Sam Bartram was warmly applauded at Fratton Park, his spectacular goalkeeping preventing the Portsmouth tally reaching double figures… Ufton did not give much scope to Vaughan [recently transferred from Charlton] but there were some near misses and grand saves from all the other home forwards.'

Bob Pennington wrote in the *Daily Express*, 'Dinner companions on the Portsmouth–London train included two opponents, Charlton goalkeeper Sam Bartram and Portsmouth centre forward Charlie Vaughan. "Thought I'd beaten you with a header right at the end," said Vaughan. "I reckon you didn't even see the ball though you pushed it over the bar." "Saw it, Saw it!" snorted Sam. "Of course I saw it. I couldn't have YOU, an old Charlton man scoring against us." "Confidentially," said Vaughan, in an aside to a companion, "Sam made a great save."'

A week before, *Soccer Star* magazine carried an article by Ken Matthews headed 'Tribute for Sam?', suggesting 'What a wonderful, fitting tribute it would be if the selectors chose Charlton Athletic's Sam Bartram for the job of keeping goal in the Great Britain team that meets the Rest of the World at Wembley, later this month. The choice is not merely sentiment on my part. He gets my vote on merit. There are few more dependable goalkeepers in the game today.' In the event Sam didn't get selected but must have been overjoyed that his teammate centre half Derek Ufton did.

In November Sam kept goal for London in Germany against Berlin. Fulham centre forward Bedford Jezzard scored a hat-trick in a 4-0 victory. The teams were; Berlin: Wittke (Union 06); Deinert (Tennis-Borussia), Strehlow (Union 06); Muller (BSV 92), Kohna (Tennis-Borussia), Herrmann (BSV 92); Wax (Union 06), Herrmann (Minerva 93), Karlsch (BSV 92), Paul (BSV 92), Sendrowski (BSV 92). London: Sam Bartram (Charlton Athletic); Alf Ramsey (Tottenham Hotspur), Stan Willemse (Chelsea); Alex Forbes (Arsenal), Harry Clarke (Tottenham Hotspur), Cyril Hammond (Charlton Athletic); Tommy Southren (West Ham), Jimmy Logie (Arsenal), Bedford Jezzard (Fulham), Roy Bentley (Chelsea), George Robb (Tottenham Hotspur).

After the 1-2 scoreline at Sunderland in December, the *News of the World* carried the headline, 'A CASE OF BARTRAM *V.* SUNDERLAND.' A week later after a 0-2 defeat by Burnley, the *Sunday Sketch* announced, 'BARTRAM AT HIS BEST. It was Burnley, Burnley all the way in the match against Charlton at Turf Moor and once again only the brilliance of Sam Bartram saved Jimmy Seed's men from a crushing defeat. Sam was beaten once in each half… but time after time he stopped shots from a flat-out Burnley attack. Burnley took command from the off and in the first minute the ever-agile Bartram made a great save when he pushed a swerving shot from Holden over the bar. And so it went on throughout the first half with Sam stopping shots from all angles.' A Burnley director commented, 'Find eleven players with the spirit of Sam Bartram and England won't have to worry any more.'

On Boxing Day another journey to Lancashire saw Charlton succumb to Bolton's unbeaten home record, going down 1–3, but Sam was headline news once again. 'BARTRAM STARS FOR CHARLTON,' said the *Sunday Dispatch*. 'Charlton's star was Sam Bartram in goal, who made many fine saves, and Hewie and Hurst were dangerous attackers. There was only one goal in the second half. Wheeler scoring after unselfish play by Lofthouse, but this was largely due to the brilliance of Bartram.'

In February, Charlton followed their earlier 6–0 home win over Liverpool with a 3–2 victory at Anfield. 'Bartram's Great Part in Charlton Win' announced the *Sunday Dispatch*. 'Evergreen goalkeeper Sam Bartram laid the foundations for Charlton's completion of the "double" over Liverpool. The Charlton forwards revealed that essential opportunism necessary for victory, but it was Bartram's brilliant goalkeeping that defied the brilliant Liverpool attack. For three parts of the game the Liverpool forwards hammered away at the imperturbable Bartram.'

A month later the focus of the football world was directed firmly on Sam when he became the first player to make 500 Football League appearances for a single club. Just about every newspaper – and there were a good few more in those days – featured Sam's outstanding career landmark with previews, features, reports or photographs. It was one of the highest-profile occasions of football's

Cutting Portsmouth's celebration cake with the Charlton mascot and Pompey skipper Jimmy Dickinson.

pre-television age. Sam's achievement was big news and his Blackheath home was open house for press photographers. Pathé News captured the occasion for the benefit of cinema audiences.

Charlton played host to Portsmouth on Sam's big day and in those times it was unusual for anything to happen on the pitch other than the game itself. That Saturday was a marvellous exception because of a wonderful gesture by Portsmouth FC. Before the kick-off a simple table from The Valley club room was placed on the playing area and topped with a large iced cake in the shape of a soccer pitch. On the top were model footballers in Charlton and Portsmouth colours. Then two of England's most popular players, Pompey skipper Jimmy Dickinson and Charlton's captain for the day Sam Bartram, were welcomed onto the pitch by the crowd, posed for photographs and cut the cake. No fireworks, no hype, just a simple ceremony that said so much and was made possible by the outstanding gift from old adversaries Portsmouth. Also, in a private presentation after the game, the Pompey chairman gave Sam an inscribed tankard to mark the occasion.

That evening and next morning the newspapers were full of the goings on at The Valley. Headlines ranged from 'Bartram's day – Charlton win' and 'He's Still the Same Sam and No Retiring' to 'A Piece of Cake for Majestic Sam' and 'The Corks Pop for Bartram.' The *People* led with 'GOOD OLD SAM KEPT CHARLTON FANS HAPPY, TOO. In case it had escaped your notice, I can now reveal that it was loyal Sam Bartram's jamboree day. Charlton's pin-up goalkeeper was making, as perhaps you'd heard, his 500th league appearance for his one and only professional club. And was duly elected "spin up" man to mark the event. The festivities included a match against Portsmouth – a quite rousing, if somewhat puzzling affair. It was a match that Portsmouth could have won if they had taken their chance and, of course, if the faithful Sam had not been in his top form.'

The *Sunday Pictorial* said, 'Sam Bartram pulled out twenty years of goalkeeping tricks for his 500th league match with Charlton – and the 37,508 crowd just cheered and cheered. They enjoyed the Bartram super show even if Portsmouth didn't. Half a dozen saves in the first half must have been some of his greatest ever.'

The *Sunday Express* even ran a stopwatch account of that very special afternoon. '2.30: Sam reads through the scores of telegrams and goodwill messages from every part of England. 3.00: The first cheer as Sam and Jimmy Dickinson, the Portsmouth captain, walk on to the field to be photographed with the special cake Portsmouth have baked. This giant confection is 3ft by 2ft and depicts a green pitch with players in Charlton and Portsmouth colours. Sam is kissed by an excited supporter who hands him a bunch of bananas. 3.12: Another salvo of cheers and Bartram wins the toss. 3.15-4.00: The first half. After a nervous start Sam gave us goalkeeping in the grand manner. Three saves – two from young Rodney Henwood, playing his first

An after-match kiss
from daughter Moira.

Helen, Moira, Sam and his mother Mary celebrate.

Left and below: Sam's 500th league game is front-page news.

Opposite: Newspaper cartoons mark Sam's 500th league game.

league match at outside left, the other a point-blank one from Harris – were world class. Portsmouth were the better side this half, but Charlton scored the only goal – a beautiful drive by Eddie Firmani. 4.10–4.55: Second half – in the best Charlton attack so far Firmani crossed a rocket centre and Stuart Leary headed home first time – a brilliant goal. Portsmouth came back and Barnard scrambled the ball in with Bartram on the ground – 2–1. Bartram's unorthodox methods – often he advanced to the edge of the penalty area, and once he booted the ball off Harris's toe – were to give heart failure. Leary made sure for Charlton when he flicked the ball into the net, right under the groping fingers of Gill, Portsmouth's 'keeper. Henderson, Harris and Reid were outstanding for Pompey. Hewie, Leary, Firmani and, of course, Bartram starred for Charlton. 5.05: Scene: the Charlton dressing room, packed with Pompey and Charlton players, club officials, and movie cameramen. The corks pop and we drink Sam's health in champagne. Jimmy Seed, the Charlton manager, makes a speech. Harry Wain, Portsmouth director, hands Sam a silver tankard and says, amid laughter; "We all hope you'll play for another 500 years." Sam, a little dazed, but obviously delighted, thanks everyone, but particularly the Charlton trainer, Jimmy Trotter, "for keeping him so clear from serious injury." It is all very moving and fitting. For players like Sam Bartram, captain for the day and best uncapped goalkeeper in the country, are the salt of soccer – one-club men whose loyalty and dedication to physical fitness are an example to all those footloose footballers who put the pounds first and the performance last. As I left the Charlton

"Hold on just a moment, he's still reading his telegrams."

dressing room, with its cheering players, their glasses held aloft, I saw written on the wall in large capitals: "Well played, Sam." AND SO SAY ALL OF US…'

For Sam the day was one of his most cherished memories. He received 150 telegrams of congratulation and still found time to send one of his own to Brian Ronson, a North-Eastern teenager, making his debut in goal for Fulham the same day. Most importantly, in the crowd was his biggest fan, Sam's mother Mary Bartram, who had travelled overnight by train from Boldon Colliery to be at the match.

David Pilditch of *Soccer Star* recalls that the following day on BBC radio's *Mr Ross and Mr Ray Show*, jazz musician Ray Ellington announced to band leader Edmundo Ross, 'Mr Ross, this is your 100th performance on the air. You're the Sam Bartram of music.'

Among the many personal messages Sam received was this one from a gentleman in Liverpool:

Sam Bartram 'The Great',
Charlton AFC, London
(The First Letter I have ever written to a sportsman)

Dear Mr Bartram,

Allow me to offer my congratulations upon your wonderful playing record of 500 appearances for Charlton AFC.

I have been a very keen follower of Liverpool since 1916 and have seen the finest goalkeepers in the game since that time – Hardy, Campbell, Elisha Scott, Ted Taylor, Sandy Mutch, Tim Williamson, Goodchild, Scattergood, Ewart, Hibbs, Swift, Farquarson, Merrick and others too numerous to mention.

I have never seen greater than you during that time and, although you have many times – as recently as a fortnight ago – thwarted my favourites you have given me great pleasure through the years. It is always a joy and thrill to see you and I have not missed one of your appearances on Merseyside through the whole of your career. As a matter of fact I did get out of a sick bed to see you play at Anfield recently and did myself no good – but I would not miss your presence for anything.

As one who played goal for a well-known amateur team for several seasons I claim to know something of goalkeeping and your sure handling, agility and anticipation have thrilled me – and many others – and many saves have astounded me by their quickness. You are a great personality and fine sportsman and I am sure your play is an inspiration to your colleagues as indeed it was in that memorable cup final – which I witnessed when you beat Burnley 1-0 by the Duffy goal. I am sure Burnley would only have scored over your dead body that day. The game is all too short of men of your character and personality, people who stay contented with one club.

Long may you reign and I hope to see you again on Merseyside several times again before you think of retiring.

All good wishes and every happiness to you as you have given it to others. I hope you get that 'cap'.

Yours sincerely,
H. Alwyn Thomas

March also saw Sam chosen for the Football Combination to meet the Dutch national XI in Amsterdam. The full team selection was: Sam Bartram (Charlton Athletic); John Hewie (Charlton Athletic), Ken Green (Birmingham City); Bob Morton (Luton Town), Syd Owen (Luton Town), Bill Dickson (Chelsea); Harry Hooper (West Ham), Jimmy Logie (Arsenal), Bedford Jezzard (Fulham), Johnny Haynes (Fulham), Denis Foreman (Brighton).

The honours were coming thick and fast for forty-year-old Sam. On the eve of the 1954 FA Cup final he played in an England trial at Highbury, the line-up for which constituted a glittering Who's Who of 1950s English football. Sam kept goal for the England XI that beat Young England 2-1. The England goal-scorers were Wilf Mannion and Tommy Lawton. Derek Hines was on target for Young England. The teams on duty at Highbury that late April evening were: England XI; Sam Bartram (Charlton Athletic); Bert Mozley (Derby County), Laurie Smith (Arsenal); Harry Johnston (Blackpool), Leon Leuty (Notts County), Henry Cockburn (Manchester United); Stanley Matthews (Blackpool), Wilf Mannion (Middlesbrough), Tommy Lawton (Arsenal), Len Shackleton (Sunderland), Bobby Langton (Blackburn Rovers). Young England: Nigel Sims (Wolverhampton Wanderers); Peter Sillett (Chelsea), Roger Byrne (Manchester United); Jimmy Adamson (Burnley), Trevor Smith (Birmingham City), Duncan Edwards (Manchester United); Tommy Hooper (West Ham), Albert Quixall (Sheffield Wednesday), Derek Hines (Leicester City), Dennis Viollet (Manchester United), Brian Pilkington (Burnley). A crowd of 43,544 watched the match in which Sam and centre half Leon Leuty, who had played on opposite sides in the 1946 cup final, were the England XI's only uncapped players.

Although Charlton fell at the first hurdle in the cup that season, losing 2-3 to Portsmouth, Sam and the Addicks will have had an eye on Wembley when West Bromwich Albion met Preston North End in the final. In goal for Albion, the 3-2 cup winners, was Jim Sanders, a former Bartram understudy, signed by Jimmy Seed from Kent club Longlands in the early 1940s. Sanders played 45 war-time matches and 1 postwar League game for Charlton before moving to West Bromwich in November 1945.

Jim Sanders FA Cup winners' medal meant an unusual triple was created, setting a tough teaser for sports quiz enthusiasts. Namely, which three FA Cup winning goalkeepers played for Charlton in March 1940? Answer: Frank Swift (Manchester City 1934), Sam Bartram (Charlton 1947) and Jim Sanders (WBA 1954).

However, Charlton did carry off one cup that season and Sam had the honour of collecting it. London daily newspaper the *Evening Standard* introduced a five-a-side competition for the capital's clubs and Charlton came out on top. George Whiting, reporting the event in the *Standard*, said, 'Charlton Athletic are the five-a-side champions of London. And if you think that is an achievement of small merit or little endeavour, you should have heard the reception they got from the enthusiastic 8,000 crowd at the Empress Hall, Earls Court, when goal-keeper Sam Bartram led his men up for their cup and medals at the end of the *Evening Standard* tournament.

Charlton's team of Sam Bartram, Cyril Hammond, John Hewie, Stuart Leary and Billy Kiernan beat Fulham, Brentford and Tottenham to carry off the trophy. In the final, the *Evening Standard* added, 'George Robb strove mightily to put Spurs in the picture, but goalkeeper Bartram had got the hang of the thing by now. Some of his saves at this period were as spectacular as anything shown us by the gymnasts who had contorted for our entertainment during the interval.'

Two weeks later in mid-May, Sam teamed up with Stanley Matthews again, this time for an exhibition match on the island of Jersey. They were invited to play as guests for the Jersey Saturday League representative team against Bournemouth. The prospect of two of the country's most popular players in action in the Channel Islands produced great excitement. The *Jersey Evening Post* announced, 'Tomorrow's Game. English Team Arrives. The Bournemouth and Boscombe Athletic team to meet the Saturday Football League at Springfield tomorrow evening arrived by air this morning, accompanied by the club's officials. The visitors already knew that they would be opposing Sam Bartram and Stanley Matthews tomorrow and were of the unanimous opinion that it was a splendid

Sam with Stanley Matthews in Jersey, May 1954.

Sam (centre back row) and Stanley Matthews (left centre) in the Jersey League XI.

idea in obtaining these two celebrated players to appear in the local XI and said their presence would greatly add to the attraction of the game. Later Mr Sam Bartram flew in by air from Northolt, and was welcomed by Mr A.M. Perredes, a vice-president of the Saturday Football League, in addition to Messrs Feltham and Olliver. Mr Bartram stated that this was his first visit to the island and he was looking forward with great keenness to the match and to playing with the local players... Stanley Matthews will arrive tomorrow morning by air.'

Under the heading 'TWO VERY GREAT FOOTBALLERS. Some Facts about Stan Matthews and Sam Bartram,' were very extensive pen-pictures of both players. To quote briefly from each, 'Nobody who has seen Matthews will ever forget his play, and there are few backs who can claim to have had the better of this fantastic footballer. Matthews, even at thirty-nine, is still a genius on the football field, and though without doubt the footballer of the past half century, there could not be one more modest about his achievements. Twenty years in football as goalkeeper of one of the most successful clubs in England, Sam Bartram of Charlton Athletic has notched a name for himself in soccer circles as being the greatest uncapped custodian ever.'

The match report in the *Jersey Evening Post* was headed, 'NEARLY 9,000 SEE GRAND FOOTBALL EXHIBITION. Saturday League Initiative Well Rewarded. Stanley Matthews and Sam Bartram Help Home Side to Splendid Victory. The report began, 'The artistry of the legendary Stanley Matthews, a first-class demonstration of goalkeeping from renowned Sam Bartram, coupled with a showing of fast progressive soccer from Bournemouth and Boscombe Athletic, and much-above-average performances from the local players, combined to make the game in which the Saturday Football League beat Bournemouth by the odd goal in five at Springfield on Saturday evening, one of the most outstanding from all viewpoints ever to have been played in Jersey. The great crowd thrilled in anticipation every time the great Matthews was in possession, and they were not disappointed… when Neave gave Siddall an opportunity the inside right was only prevented from scoring by Bartram making a top-class save, to an appreciative roar from the crowd. A powerful shot from Siddall led to Bartram saving again, the ball spinning out of his hands, but the 'keeper quickly recovered possession and threw it clear. It was noticeable that nearly all Bartram's clearances were made by accurate and strong throws – very often to Matthews.'

Such was the enthusiasm at the ground after the game, with hundreds of people outside the dressing rooms, that Sam and Stan had to be smuggled out of the stadium by police and driven away in a fast car with fans in hot pursuit. When they arrived at their hotel they were met by a large group of schoolboys waiting patiently for autographs in the pouring rain. The players obliged and the lads left wet but happy. At a celebration dinner that evening Sam and Stan were given silver tankards in the shape of a Jersey milk can, as souvenirs of their visit.

The pair had played together for England against Wales at Wembley in 1940 and would have been teammates before then had Jimmy Seed succeeded in signing Matthews from Stoke City in the 1930s. Many managers were after the boy wonder's signature at the time. Seed may well have got his man but Charlton were not prepared to pay Stoke's asking price. After the war Stan moved to Blackpool, for whom he played in three FA Cup finals, including the epic 4-3 victory over Bolton in 1953. His return to the Potteries in 1961 brought a rejuvenation of his home-town club. He helped Stoke climb back to the First Division and played at that level until the age of fifty. In 1965 Stanley Matthews became the first professional footballer to be knighted.

In May 1954 Sam was part of Charlton's pioneering tour to South America. The scheduled six-match visit began at Bogotá in Columbia. On arrival it was apparent that the facilities provided fell below what was promised. Major administrative problems also threatened the success of the trip. The first 2 matches against Millionarios and Sante Fe were both 2-2 draws. There were ugly scenes in the next game and after a disagreement with the organisers Charlton were forced to travel on to Peru and Ecuador. Two matches in Peru resulted in defeats but in an additional match in Guayaquil, Ecuador, Charlton met Spanish club Barcelona and won 3-2.

The effects of playing at altitude and other local hazards resulted in many of the party, the club doctor included, becoming ill. The situation was so serious that Sam phoned home in desperation to ask his wife Helen to contact the club in London for assistance. Eventually the party arrived home safely and Charlton made a financial surplus from the tour. However the club unsuccessfully contested for other monies due from the organisers for many years thereafter.

The tour rounded off a momentous year for Sam, who was runner-up to Tom Finney in the voting for Footballer of the Year and during the summer Charlton extended the Landsdown Mews turnstiles, high above the vast east terrace, and renamed this area The Sam Bartram Entrance in honour of their famous long-serving goalkeeper. This was surely the most spectacular approach to a football ground anywhere in the country. Once through the turnstiles, The Valley spread out before you, like the territory of a bird of prey seen from the air. The distinctive arch-roofed grandstand opposite was a scale model of itself and acres of open terracing descended steeply to the pitch far below.

When the new season began at Bolton in August 1954, former international 'keeper Frank Swift wrote in the *News of the World*, 'Sam Bartram is in terrific form again this season. In this game at Bolton he pulled a thigh muscle midway through the second half. Then somebody stood on his fingers. But he defied all these misfortunes and the whole Bolton team at the same time. Nat Lofthouse too hit the form which makes him a "must" for the England team. Only some staggering saves by Bartram stopped Nat from running away with the game.' Praise indeed from the giant goalkeeper who, for so long, had prevented Sam from breaking into the full England team.

After the same match, Peter Brooke wrote in the *Sunday Express*, 'Bartram made himself the man of the match when, in three minutes, he saved shots and

Above left: Eddie Firmani watches Sam beat Huddersfield Town's Jimmy Glazzard.

Above right: A magnificent magazine photo of Sam turning a shot to safety.

headers from every Bolton forward in turn.' At the end of the game Sam received an ovation from the Burnden Park crowd and congratulatory handshakes from many of the Bolton team.

Two weeks later Charlton were in the North-West again, this time at Old Trafford and Sam was headline news. 'SAM SAVES CHARLTON FROM BIG HIDING,' announced the *Sunday Dispatch*, adding 'Sam Bartram gave another of his outstanding performances. But for the forty-year-old Charlton goalkeeper's efforts this would have been a complete rout. The match became a battle between the United forward line and Sam. Bartram was in action in the first minute and saved at least three goals before Rowley put his side ahead in the fifteenth minute… The United forwards were constantly attacking and young Viollet, inside left, must still be wondering what magic powers this man Bartram possesses.'

Despite Sam's heroics, Charlton went down 2-3 at Bolton and 1-3 at Manchester United. He was cheered by the Old Trafford crowd as he left the pitch and Jimmy Seed is on record as saying that without Bartram's brilliant display United might have scored ten.

The team's form was erratic until mid-season when 12 wins and 2 draws were recorded in 18 outings. During this period Eddie Firmani claimed four hat-tricks, including five goals in a 6-1 win over Aston Villa at The Valley. The South African, who made his club debut in 1951, was having his best season and his 26 goals from 39 appearances made him hot property. Next summer he moved to Italian club Sampdoria for £35,000, a record fee for a British-based player. Firmani later played for Inter Milan, Genoa and Italy, before returning twice to Charlton as a player, then manager.

In the FA Cup, Sam and company had only managed one win since Charlton lost their grip on the trophy at Huddersfield in 1948. This time round a 3-1 away victory over Rochdale and a 4-2 home success at the expense of West Bromwich Albion gave cause for optimism, especially as these had been the club's first two scalps in their 1947 cup-winning run, but the subsequent away draw at Wolverhampton proved more than the Addicks could handle. High-flying Wolves, who had already completed the double over Charlton in the league, also eased home 4-1 at snow-covered Molineux in the cup.

In the tie with FA Cup holders West Bromwich at The Valley, Sam saved a Ronnie Allen penalty kick in dramatic fashion. With the score at 0-0, the England centre forward's spot kick was beaten out by Bartram, who was then hit in the face by Allen's follow-up shot, sending the ball over the bar to safety. Derek Ufton tells the story that, as the players gathered round their goalkeeper lying prostrate on the pitch, Sam looked up and said jokingly, 'There, I told you I was one of the best headers of the ball in the game!'

Minutes later, Charlton were awarded a penalty. Eddie Firmani took the kick, which was saved by Albion 'keeper Reg Davies but this time Firmani followed up to score. The *Sunday Dispatch* proclaimed, 'Evergreen goalkeeper Sam Bartram and Young England centre forward Bobby Ayre are the heroes of Charlton. Bartram made two out-of-this-world saves that loosened West Bromwich Albion's grip on the cup they won at Wembley last year. Ayre administered the knock-out blow with a brilliant second-half hat-trick.'

After the 1-2 league defeat at Wolves, the *Sunday Express* claimed, 'Happy Sam inspires Charlton.' Reporter Edwin Buckley wrote, 'Greetings Sam Bartram, on your forty-first birthday. For most of your twenty-two years you have been visiting Molineux but you can never have given such a wonderful a display as you did on your birthday, when you defied Wolves in their most ravenous mood. For nearly an hour this wonderful red-headed Geordie brought out saves with speed and agility that had the crowd roaring. Players like Hancocks and Swinbourne more than once stood amazed as their goal-scoring drives were pushed round the post or tipped one-handed over the bar.'

The *Sunday Pictorial* added, 'Better-than-ever, evergreen Sam Bartram emerged from the slog and sweat as a mud-stained hero. He celebrated his forty-first birthday with a goalkeeping performance that earned an ovation from even the most partisan Wolves' supporters.'

In their report of the league game at Roker Park, Sunderland, the *News of the World* led with, 'AND SAM WAS BORN IN SUNDERLAND TOO!' and continued, 'Sam Bartram went home to his birthplace, Sunderland, yesterday, and personally saw to it that his home-town team's unbeaten ground record was shattered. He put on a magnificent show, standing up under terrific Sunderland pressure, saved a penalty, and was only beaten one minute from the end, when Shackleton put one past him.' Charlton's 2-1 win at Roker Park in February was their last of the season. A disappointing run of results saw them finish in the bottom half of the league table.

In April, after a 2-2 draw at Everton on a Saturday, the team flew to Spain for a friendly game with Real Madrid the following day. Time was short so the dirty kit from Goodison Park accompanied the players, who arrived in Madrid on Sunday morning. Sam and his colleagues were amazed when their Spanish hosts delivered the team strip freshly laundered and boots cleaned and dubbined, ready for the afternoon kick-off. Just two days later, on a Tuesday afternoon, the Addicks were at home to Manchester United in a rearranged First Division fixture. There were no floodlights at Charlton then, so in the space of exactly four days, Sam and his colleagues faced Everton, Real Madrid and Manchester United.

Season 1955/56 began in a heatwave with Sam reckoning he lost half a stone in weight at The Valley during the 2-2 opening-day draw with Luton, who were playing in the top flight for the first time. 'It was the hottest match I have ever played in,' he claimed. A couple of days later, at Bramall Lane, Sheffield, he was as cool as ever as Charlton claimed a 0-0 draw. 'BARTRAM TURNS IN ANOTHER GREAT SHOW' was the *Daily Sketch* headline. 'Bartram again. For more than

Charlton Athletic, First Division 1955/56. Back row: Cyril Hammond, Jock Campbell, Sam Bartram, John Hewie, Don Townsend, Derek Ufton. Front row: Gordon Hurst, Jimmy Gauld, Stuart Leary, Ronnie White, Billy Kiernan.

twenty years sandy-haired Sam has been playing great stuff in the Charlton goal and on his showing against Sheffield United at Bramall Lane last night Sam's good for many more seasons. He saved everything that Joe Mercer's boys threw at him – and that was plenty… Sam Bartram, the Stanley Matthews of goalkeepers, should get paid time and a half. He alone prevented Sheffield United presenting new manager Joe Mercer with his first two points of the season. Among his many brilliant saves he included one from the penalty spot eight minutes from time.'

Three straight wins followed at Bolton, at home to Sheffield United and away at Tottenham, with Charlton scoring three goals each time. In October a 6-1 win over Portsmouth at The Valley was followed by a 4-2 victory against Arsenal at Highbury. The next game resulted in a 5-2 win at home to Manchester City with Jim Ryan scoring four times. The Addicks were certainly scoring goals – three or more followed against Aston Villa, Huddersfield, Bolton, Manchester United and West Bromwich – but they were unable to find any consistency.

In the third round of the cup, non-league Burton Albion visited The Valley. The independent Burton website *Brewersnet* recalls that 'in only their sixth season of football, the Brewers had climbed the mountain that all non-league clubs aspire to, and reached the third round of the FA Cup. There awaiting them were one of the top teams in the country at the time – Charlton Athletic – including among their ranks legendary goalkeeper Sam Bartram. Four London-bound "Football Special" trains were laid on from Burton to take the amber-and-black-clad fans to The Valley. It was unquestionably the biggest day in the club's short history, and the fact that Albion received a 7-0 thrashing from the mighty Robins barely detracted from the occasion for the Brewers fans in a 29,000 crowd.'

Swindon Town were beaten 2-1 in the fourth round, setting up a plum home tie with Arsenal in the fifth round. The match produced more interest than any of Charlton's cup games since the 1940s, with the away win at Highbury in October providing extra spice to the occasion. Not that any was needed for a first-ever FA Cup meeting with Arsenal. A 72,000 crowd packed The Valley and many more watched the highlights on cinema newsreels the following week. Unfortunately for Charlton things went Arsenal's way this time and a 2-0 win took the Highbury club into the quarter-finals.

A few weeks later came the news that Sam had been appointed manager of York City. He was offered and accepted the post on Friday 9 March and played his last game for Charlton the very next day. Appropriately, Arsenal were the visitors to The Valley and, just as on his 450th league appearance, Sam had the honour of leading out the Charlton team to meet the Gunners. Many of the 40,000 crowd that afternoon, whichever team they favoured, had never seen Charlton play without Sam Bartram in goal.

Indeed the same must have applied to plenty of the parents of those present. Everyone knew, especially Sam, that there would come a time when someone else would take over the 'keeper's jersey. The sudden arrival of that moment came as a surprise, even to Charlton Athletic's beloved goalkeeper. He had turned down the opportunity to become York's player-manager three years earlier. Now at forty-two, although still super fit, the chance to manage his second favourite club was too good to miss.

Almost exactly two years after his 500th league game, Sam was the focus of major media attention once again. On Saturday 10 March, as the familiar strains of Billy Cotton and his band echoed from the speakers in The Valley stand, the clicking of studs filled the concrete-based tunnel leading to the pitch. Helen and Moira Bartram looked down from above the players' entrance, the fans sprang to their feet and a smiling Sam trotted out, followed by his red-shirted colleagues, to face twenty or more photographers eager to capture the moment.

In his autobiography Sam recalls, 'I was almost knocked over by the deafening blast of the cheering from the crowd… its volume and warmth took me by surprise. I have heard some loud cheering at The Valley over the years, but I can honestly say this beat everything.' The captains tossed for ends. Sam and Arsenal's Cliff Holton, who had played together for London, watched the coin fall. Sam then turned away and headed for his goal, pursued by cameramen, some in trilby hats and long coats, snapping away with flashbulbs popping.

There was no doubt that he was playing as well as ever and had the offer of an attractive managerial job not come along, Sam would have continued in Charlton's goal for some time. Looking back, it's heart-warming that he was able to go out at the top and in style! Determined not to allow Arsenal to score in his

Left: Captain for the day, Sam greets Arsenal skipper Cliff Holton.

Below: Cameramen race for position as Sam takes his place in goal.

Above and right: Sam keeps a
clean sheet.

final game, Sam led Charlton to a 2-0 victory and the Addicks' first ever 'double'
over their long-term rivals.

As he left the field, youngsters rushed on to congratulate him and for once it
was an emotional Sam who tried to address the adoring crowd from the stand.
Draped in a towel, he took the microphone, just as he had as a young man twenty
years before when promotion to the First Division was celebrated, and again the
words failed him. It didn't matter, his actions over twenty-two years said it all and
it was common knowledge that Sam loved Charlton and Charlton loved Sam.

On emerging from the players' and officials' entrance at the rear of the stand, which
resembled a domestic front door in the Bartram era, Sam was besieged by hordes of
admiring autograph hunters. Nothing unusual about that, except on this occasion
the time needed to fulfil all the requests took longer than his regular journey home.

The famous French newspaper *France-Soir* summed up the occasion with, 'Les
adieux de Bartram' ('Bartram's Farewell'). 'At forty-two years of age, Sam Bartram,

Above: Newspapers report Sam's last Charlton appearance.

Left: Sam addresses the crowd.

Charlton's goalkeeper for more than a quarter of a century, retired from the game last Saturday. For his final match he kept a clean sheet, and Charlton beat Arsenal by two goals to nil. The demonstration that followed the match was the most emotional that a stadium has ever witnessed. Bartram, acclaimed by all Charlton's supporters, had to make a short speech before the microphone, and all his admirers then sang in chorus *Auld Lang Syne*. I reverently raise my hat to a career such as Bartram's. It honours the name of Sport just as much as Lord Burghley's did. Moreover, if men are to be judged by the love they show for the game, then let us say once and for all that we find these stories about "Amateurs" and "Professionals" quite ridiculous. Authentic, good-hearted Sportsmen belong to each category, and Bartram is a true Sportsman, a Sportsman without reproach.'

A supporter's letter also expressed similar feelings: 'Well, I could not refrain from feeling a soccer lump in my throat as you said goodbye to the multitudinous

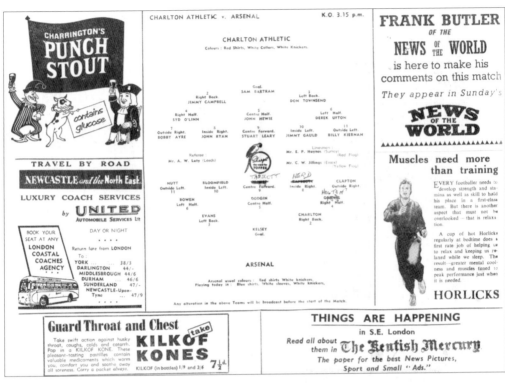

The name Bartram appears in the Charlton line-up for the last time.

Fans salute their hero.

Left: From *Football Monthly,* June 1956.

Opposite left: Monday 12 March: Sam playres for Ex-Millwall XI in John Short's testimonial.

Opposite, above right: Saturday 10 March: Sam's last match for Charlton.

Opposite, below right: Wednesday 14 March: Sam's first match as manager of York City.

well-wishers of yours on the playing pitch at Charlton on Saturday. Soccer is all the better for such a man as you are, on the field and off the field, always a sports-man and a nature's gentleman and ye gods, twenty-two years! I could see that you were near breaking point with the thousands cheering you when you came into the Directors' Box to say au revoir, if not goodbye. I am only one of the thousands of people who wish you well…'

Two days after he left The Valley, Sam began his managerial role at a meeting of Football League clubs in London. That evening he appeared in a testimonial match for John Short of Millwall. Fortunately this gave his admirers another chance to wish him well, especially those who had missed his swift departure from Charlton on Saturday. So on Monday 12 March Sam lined-up against an All Star XI for a team of former Millwall players at The Den, New Cross. He qualified by having played as a guest for Millwall in the 1945 wartime cup semi-final and final. Sam's only playing colleague from these games on view was left-back George Fisher, although inside left Willie Hurrell had been reserve for both teams in the final!

The full ex-Millwall XI was: Sam Bartram; Des Quinn, George Fisher; Frank Reeves, Gerry Bowler, John Short; Ronnie Mansfield, Willie Hurrell, Frank Neary, Stan Morgan, Johnny Hartburn. This was the first of many testimonial and exhibition matches Sam took part in over the following years. He was much in demand and regularly took the opportunity to support players' testimonial events or other fundraising projects.

Meanwhile, the Charlton goalkeeper's jersey was appropriately inherited by Frank Reed, another County Durham lad who, like Sam, was a product of

Sunderland Schools' football. He was signed from Murton Colliery, the club who were on the wrong end of a Bartram hat-trick on Sam's Easington Colliery debut a quarter of a century earlier. The six-foot-four-inch Reed had moved to The Valley at the start of the season. He made his league debut when Charlton next took the field for a First Division game, an afternoon fixture with Manchester City at Maine Road on 21 March. Frank kept a clean sheet in a 2-0 win.

In the programme for the subsequent home game at The Valley was this message: 'In a message from York, Sam Bartram requests us to thank his legion of fans at Charlton for their kind letters and good wishes. Sam will always be remembered at Charlton and we shall watch his career on the managerial side with great interest. Totting up the figures the other day we found that Sam made exactly 800 first-team appearances in goal for Charlton.'

To anyone following soccer since the Bartram days, the game seems to have moved smoothly from one decade to another with very few radical changes. It's

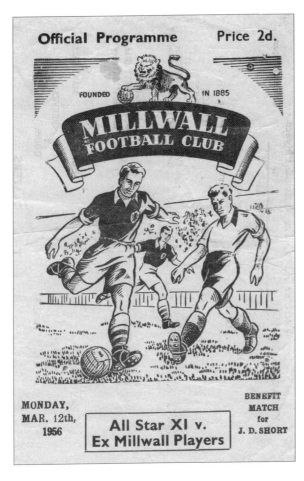

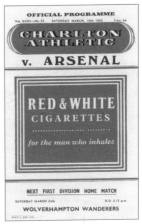

Icy conditions as a mobile Bartram thwarts Blackburn in February 1947.

only when looking back from the distance of half a century or so, to the days when Sam was patrolling the penalty area and sometimes more besides, that it really becomes apparent how very different things are today.

When he became a full-time player in 1934, there was no televised football and very little live coverage on radio. There was hardly any marketing of the game as we have come to accept now, yet in the inter-war years crowds followed the game in their hundreds of thousands. Spectators were not segregated and seating provision at most grounds was minimal. Communication with the public was often made by carrying a chalked board around the touchline. Before a Stoke City *v.* Charlton match in 1937 a notice was carried round the ground announcing that railway breakdown gangs were needed urgently. A total of 33,007 fans had paid to enter the ground. There was no mention of how many left without watching the game!

Identification of players was made by their position on the field. Standard numbering of teams was not introduced until the late 1930s. From that time jerseys were numbered 2 to 11 and a set of shirts lasted all season. There were no substitutes and injured players were often obliged to continue the game as 'passengers', sometimes despite serious injury and were usually banished to the wing. There were no isotonic drinks then, the only mid-game refreshment available was a drenching from the trainer's cold wet sponge.

Goalkeepers invariably wore green sweaters; red, blue and white were the other colours allowed. Yellow was used only in internationals and other representative

No numbers were worn in Sam's early days at Charlton.

matches. Numbering of goalkeepers was not generally introduced until the 1970s and jerseys were of a single colour. There were no designer patterns until more recent times.

Red and yellow cards for referees were not invented until 1966, so disciplined players' names were simply entered into the referee's notebook. Sendings-off for more serious offences were rare. The match ball was often left on the centre spot during the half-time interval. Managers sat well away from the action and were rarely seen by the majority of the crowd.

Despite the lack of segregation, football crowds were generally good humoured. Motor cars were a luxury and rail journeys took longer, so away fans did not travel in great numbers, except for cup ties, where the friendly banter between rival fans was often a feature. There were no replica shirts then but fans often wore their team's colours in the form of woollen scarves and, for important games, a coloured favour or rosette, sometimes bearing the team's name. Singing was not part of the atmosphere, apart from the famous 'Pompey Chimes' and 'On the Ball, Norwich City'. The Kop, at Liverpool, changed all that in the 1960s.

A popular fundraising venture at some grounds was 'Penny on the Ball'. Fans bought a numbered ticket for one penny before the game, a draw took place and the winning number was displayed on a board taken around the pitch at half-time. Following the match the proud winner collected the ball that his idols had just been playing with, from the club office. What a prize!

Kick-off times were generally earlier, especially in mid season, as there were no floodlights. At holiday times matches were often played in the morning and mid-week games usually in the afternoon. Most people worked Saturday mornings, so had limited time to get to games and indeed would have to take time off to follow their team in midweek. Other than for local derbies, following your team to away venues was often out of the question.

Teams usually travelled to away matches by train and coach ('charabanc', to quote Jimmy Seed). Individual players used public transport to get to and from home matches. If there was a large crowd this could present a problem. There is a story of Charlton players having to run from Woolwich to reach The Valley on time for an important match, because all the trams and buses were completely full up with fans.

Newspapers were the main medium of communication and most towns and cities published a Saturday evening sports edition, with full reports of the local games. Many of the provincial sports papers still exist, although London has not had a weekend evening newspaper for many years. At one time there were three journals seeking eager readers, the *Evening News*, *Evening Standard* and *Evening Star*. All produced classified editions, on sale within a couple of hours of the end of the game, with results, up-to-date league tables and detailed match reports. Earlier editions carried half-time scores.

Press photographers would sit close to the goal accompanied by a messenger, who would often leave early in the game to rush photographs to his newspaper by motorbike in time for publication in the evening edition. Outside cinemas, later on as the queues formed, the paper sellers would bark out football results. Star, News and Standard. All classified!' Each paper cost an old penny. For three pence you could buy the lot.

Half-time scores were displayed at grounds on scoreboards, or around the perimeter of the pitch. By using a code shown in the club's match programme, spectators could read off the scores from cricket scoreboard-style number plates, placed on the boards early in the second-half. Full-time scores, however, were

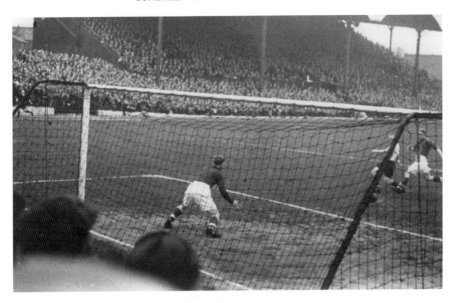

A familiar view of Sam from the terraces.

only obtained from the BBC's *Sports Report* programme between five and six o'clock, or from the classified editions of the newspapers.

It was chiefly through playing in front of large crowds, publicity in the press and on radio, plus word of mouth, that Sam and other players of his day became well known. The other very effective method of popularising football and footballers was the widespread publication of cigarette and trade cards. Quite early in his career Charlton's goalkeeper featured on a 'Topical Times' card and in the 1939 Churchman Cigarette card series. After the war, footballers also appeared on cards promoted by comics and confectionery manufacturers, so images of Sam could be found in sweet-cigarette and bubble gum packets.

Paper was at a premium for a long time in the 1940s, restricting the scale of match programmes, so lightweight four or eight-page editions were standard. Later, clubs like Arsenal and Chelsea introduced action photographs but productions were modest compared with today's glossy full-colour versions. In the 1950s fans were reading the new regular magazines, especially *Charles Buchan's Football Monthly* and Raich Carter's weekly title *Soccer Star*. Others followed as sports publishing grew more popular.

Although cup finals were shown live by the BBC from 1938, few households owned a television set then and public houses certainly didn't. The popular way to watch highlights of matches was at the cinema, where important games featured on the Pathé or Movietone newsreels. Charlton supporter Trevor Bartlett recalls queuing for over two hours at Bexleyheath in 1946 to see the Addicks on news footage from Wembley at the local cinema. 'I don't know what film was showing. I only

Jock Campbell, John Hewie, Sam Bartram and Benny Fenton with Valley groundsman Bert Chase.

went to see the cup final,' he added. Charlton's fifth round tie against Blackburn at The Valley in 1947 was the first FA Cup match, other than a final, to be televised. However, BBC's *Match of the Day* programme was not introduced until 1964.

Footballers may have graced the silver screen but they were not blessed with a film star lifestyle. Even the great Raich Carter, despite a striking likeness to Hollywood legend Charlie Chaplin, was restricted to earning just £12 per week when he became Hull City's player-manager in 1948. This was because a maximum wage existed for professionals in the Football League. Fortunately, soccer commitments encroached less into the summer months then than now and many footballers, Carter included, doubled up as county cricketers in the close season. Frank Rist, who was centre half at Charlton in Sam's early years, was a regular with Essex. Later teammates Sid O'Linn, Stuart Leary and Derek Ufton were all Kent cricketers. O'Linn also played Test match cricket for South Africa.

Doubling-up was commonplace, with England cricketers Denis Compton, Willie Watson and Arthur Milton all playing football for England, while soccer internationals Ted Drake, Raich Carter, Leslie Compton, Joe Hulme and Derek Ufton played county cricket. Even Yorkshire and England's Brian Close and Freddie Trueman, famous for their outstanding cricketing exploits, had outings for Leeds United, Arsenal, Bradford City and Lincoln City respectively.

This highlights one of the most significant differences between then and now. Then, players usually had a career prior to becoming a professional footballer, working their way up from junior soccer, and had the opportunity to pursue other employment in the summer months. Now, footballers are often recruited into the game direct from school, or through club academies and are tied to a full-time regime, with no chance to enjoy the benefits of a wider sporting experience, but they are of course considerably better recompensed for their skills. Thre is no doubt that the loyalty of their long-serving and sometimes long-suffering forebears has helped pave the way for the comforts lavished on modern footballers, both on and off the field.

It's incredible just how many things we take for granted now that were not part of life in the Bartram era. Multi-channel television, hi-fi systems, continental holidays, mobile phones and the internet came much later. Even McDonald's first British restaurant didn't open in Woolwich until 1974.

seven

INTO MANAGEMENT

On Tuesday 13 March 1956 an excited Sam set off from King's Cross on a fresh challenge. The newspapers that had so often pictured him in dramatic action shots now showed manager Bartram leaving sedately by train, as he embarked on his new career. First stop was Bradford Park Avenue where York were playing a Third Division (North) match the following afternoon.

Bradford were quick off the mark by including in their programme notes, 'Sam Bartram will be attending his first game today as York City manager. He played against us many times in wartime football for York, and all who knew him wish him well, but with our position as it is, we can hardly, even with all the goodwill in the world, hope that York will celebrate with two points today.'

At the time York were just below mid-table with 13 wins and just 7 defeats from 33 games. Park Avenue were struggling near the bottom. Sam was selected for the manager's post from over thirty applicants and granted a three-year contract. It was a popular appointment at Bootham Crescent where he played so often as a guest during the war.

The move north meant having to sell his sports business near The Valley and leaving the family at home in London. Daughter Moira had reached a crucial stage in her primary education and it was felt unwise to move schools. So for the first year and more, Sam was in York on his own but he had plenty of experience to assist him both on and off the field.

A year beforehand City had made history and taken the soccer world by surprise with an exciting brand of attacking football that saw them join the select band of Third Division clubs to reach the semi-finals of the FA Cup. They held eventual winners Newcastle to a 1-1 draw at Hillsborough, before losing the replay 0-2 at Sunderland. This run was the more remarkable because it was achieved without a manager. Secretary Billy Sherringham and trainer Tom Lockie had run things at the club since the last manager Jimmy McCormick resigned in September 1954. They were great servants of City – Sherringham was one of the club's founder

Tom Lockie's benefit game at York in April 1952. Sam and members of a Football League
XI with Tom Lockie. Len Shackleton is on the far right.

members and Lockie had been at Bootham Crescent since 1936. Sam was in a
Football League XI that played in his benefit match there in 1952. Both men
knew Sam well from his wartime affinity to York.

Although York lost 1-2 at Bradford in his first match, they finished the season in
eleventh place. Sam saw the following 1956/57 campaign as one of consolidation
and change and must have been pleased when City ended up seventh. In fact, during the season they established a new club record when they beat Southport 9-1.
One of the new players brought in was former Millwall forward Alan Monkhouse,
signed from Newcastle, but he failed to keep established striker Norman Wilkinson
out of the side. A more productive buy was midfield man Peter Wragg from Sheffield
United, who became a key player and later captain of Bartram's eleven.

At the conclusion of the 1957/58 season, Third Divisions (North) and (South)
were due to merge to form national Third and Fourth Divisions. So York's priority
that year was to finish in the top half of the Third Division (North) and become
founder members of the new Third Division. In effect they just missed out on
goal average but the FA Cup provided some highlights. A two-goal victory over
Birmingham City in the third round brought the eventual cup winners Bolton
Wanderers to York in the fourth round. Bolton drew a postwar record gate of 23,600.
City held Wanderers to a 0-0 draw at Bootham Crescent but lost the replay 0-3.

The following year Sam visited familiar territory, when York played at Millwall
and Crystal Palace, and led the club to their first ever promotion. City finished
third in the Fourth Division's inaugural season and were promoted, along with

York City Association Football and Athletic Club, Ltd.

(Members of Football League, (Division III, Northern Section) and Midland League)

Secretary:
G.W. SHERRINGTON.

Manager:
S. BARTRAM.

Phone 21447 York.
House Phone 77143 York.

Office and Ground :
BOOTHAM CRESCENT.

23 – 12 – 58

Dear Derek

Please note you are selected to play against

Doncaster

at York on Sat 27th Dec 1958

Please report at Bootham Crescent not later than 1 – 15 P.m.

~~Bus leaves ground at~~ Kick Off 2 – 15 P.m.

Won 2 – 1

Yours sincerely,

Sam Bartram

A York City selection card for a match in 1958.

Enjoying the celebrations as the National Sporting Club honour Stanley Matthews at the Café Royal London in 1956. From left to right: cricketer Jim Laker, footballers Sam Bartram, Stanley Matthews, John Charles, Trevor Ford and racing driver Mike Hawthorn.

York City's new manager is introduced to his players by skipper Ernie Phillips.

Above left: Making a presentation to Jimmy Seed in February 1957 after his retirement as Charlton manager.

Above right: Testing the York City pitch at Bootham Crescent.

Port Vale, Coventry and Shrewsbury. Unfortunately they found the new Third
Division too hot to handle and after a disappointing year were relegated in 1960.

In the summer Sam was offered the vacant manager's post at Luton Town and
York agreed to his release. In mid-July he took up his new position with the
Second Division club. The situation at Kenilworth Road bore an uncanny resem-
blance to that he encountered on his arrival at York. Luton had been cup finalists
the previous year and recently relegated from the First Division. Sam had taken
over an ageing squad.

New signings were made. Lee Spencer, a forward from Rochdale, and
Nottingham Forest winger Stewart Imlach, a member of their 1959 cup-winning
team against Luton, joined the club in August. Goalkeeper Jim Standen arrived
from Arsenal and challenged former England international Ron Baynham for
the 'keeper's jersey. Irish winger Billy Bingham moved to Everton early in the
season in exchange for inside right Alec Ashworth and full-back John Bramwell.
Left winger Jim Fleming joined from Partick Thistle in November with full-
back Joe McBride moving in the opposite direction. Outside right Harry Walden
was signed from Kettering in January. In all thirty-three players were used in the
1960/61 season. Especially frustrating for Sam will have been the need for five
goalkeepers.

Sam's first signings for Luton Town, Les Spencer (left) from Rochdale and Stewart Imlach
from Nottingham Forest.

However he must have been reasonably satisfied with his opening results, two wins and four draws in the first 8 matches. The following week took Sam on a sentimental journey to The Valley. It was an inhospitable homecoming; Charlton won 4-1 and further poor results followed. A 6-1 home victory over Middlesbrough in November contrasted starkly with a 1-7 reverse at Sunderland in December, illustrating the inconsistency of Luton's performances. One constant was the goal-scoring ability of centre forward Gordon Turner, who scored 26 League goals in 37 games.

Happily for Charlton Turner was missing when they visited Kenilworth Road but Luton avenged the earlier defeat when they reversed the tables to win 4-1. At home they were beaten only three times but fifteen away defeats restricted Sam's team to a mid-table spot. One amazing slice of luck did come their way in January. Luton trailed 2-6 at home to Manchester City in an FA Cup tie when the match was abandoned. Denis Law had scored all six City goals. When the match was replayed four days later, Luton won 3-1.

Prior to the start of the 1961/62 campaign Luton acquired experienced centre half Ron Cope from Manchester United and inside left Tommy McKechnie from Glasgow club Rob Roy. A bright start was made with a 4-1 home success over Preston and away form was much improved with three victories in the first five outings, including a 1-0 win at The Valley. Strangely, it was on their compact home ground that they were unable to better the previous year's record.

Over the season Luton's form was erratic. In the New Year a run of 4 matches produced a 5-1 home success over Swansea, a 0-3 defeat at Southampton, a 1-6 drubbing by Charlton at Kenilworth Road and a 1-0 win at Newcastle. The programme for Luton's last Second Division match of the season puts it fair and square, 'We welcome you here today for the last match of the 1961/62 season regretting that in the end it has turned out to be rather a disappointing one after the great hopes we had entertained right up to December that the fight was going well and we would still be at the top of the table when we reached this part of the programme.'

Having occupied third place in early December, Luton suffered four successive defeats without scoring a single goal. In the end they managed another respectable mid-table finish – one of eight clubs with thirty-nine points. Charlton were one of the others but with an inferior goal average.

It seems that frustration at not making a swift return to the First Division or being serious contenders for promotion – as a result of some poor performances and restricted funding for new players – caused unrest on the club's board and made Sam's situation impossible. All this forced him to resign from his post in June 1962 after only two years with the club.

Most of the football world, in which Sam had numerous friends, would have wanted him to succeed in management. He certainly didn't fail and without the disagreements at Luton, given more time and resources, might have

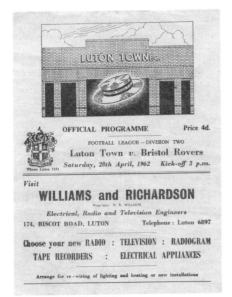

Above left: Sam's last game in management, Luton Town *v.* Bristol Rovers, April 1962.

Above right: From *Charles Buchan's Football Monthly*, August 1971.

delivered what the club craved, a return ticket to the First Division. This was no easy passage, as fellow managers at Newcastle, Sunderland, Leeds and indeed Charlton were finding.

During his time in management Sam appeared all over the country in one-off matches for players' testimonial funds and charities. It is impossible to trace all these appearances as they were many and various. Sam turned out for the Managers' XI, All Star XI, Len Shackleton's XI and Sailor Brown's Old An' New Stars XI, at places as far apart as Carlisle and Bristol in the west and Newcastle and Great Yarmouth in the east. Many famous players appeared in these games, which drew good crowds and were a feature of the early days of floodlit football. For supporters of lower-league clubs and followers of non-league soccer especially, these occasions provided a rare chance to see 'big' names in action.

Regulars alongside Sam in the All Star XI and Managers' XIs, both controlled by former Portsmouth manager Bob Jackson, were former internationals Bill Shankly, Wally Barnes, Laurie Scott, Charlie Mitten, Willie Watson and Jimmy Hagan. At Millwall in October 1956 Sam was joined in the All Star XI line-up by Raich Carter, his Sunderland Schools' skipper from 1928. Their respective pen-pictures from the match programme are worth quoting: 'SAM BARTRAM: A great favourite at The Den... Speak of Charlton Athletic and you think of Sam. Only regret is that he never received an international cap. A great goalkeeper and respected wherever football is played. RAICH CARTER: One of the great inside forwards of all

Sam and Raich Carter, colleagues for Sunderland Schoolboys, England and various testimonial matches and cup final opponents in 1946. Both progressed to management and journalism.

time. Holder of many English international caps, started his career with Sunderland and Derby County. Has received every honour that football can give.'

Below Sam's name in the programme notes for Len Shackleton's XI *v.* Showbiz XI at Brough Park Newcastle, on Sunday 3 April 1960, it states: 'Seeing he began his career at Boldon in the outfield, he has been given a run out at full-back for this game, but will probably interchange positions with Fraser. [Former Sunderland and Scotland 'keeper].' Later in the month it was a return to The Valley. Four years after his final game for the Addicks Sam was in a Charlton Old Stars XI to play the Television All Stars in aid of the United Appeal for the Blind and Stars of Spastics. The Charlton Old Stars line-up was published as, Sam Bartram; Billy Shreeve, Frank Lock; Benny Fenton, Bert Turner, Don Welsh; Gordon Hurst, 'Sailor' Brown, Charlie Vaughan, Les Boulter, Chris Duffy – some team!! The TV All Stars were from; Maurice Kaufman, Don Fox, Pete Murray,

Larry Taylor, Mike Desmond, Bernie Winters, Mike Winters, Ronnie Corbett, Jess Conrad, Andrew Ray, Harry Fowler, Roy Castle, Anthony Newley, Bernard Bresslaw, Derek Franklin, Peter Thompson and Norman (Cup Cake) Rossington – and they probably needed all of those.

That year Sam also played in an International Managers XI against the Show Biz XI, at Aldershot, in support of the Army Physical Training Corps Benevolent Fund and the Show Biz Charity Fund. Playing that day, during his pre-James Bond era, was film actor Sean Connery.

In August 1961 Sam was still playing and turned out for Sailor Brown's Old An' New Stars v. the TV All Stars at Great Yarmouth. 'Sailor' had a sports business at nearby Gorleston and among his other 'invites' were Mike Bailey (Charlton) and Billy Elliot (Sunderland). Norwich goalkeeper Ken Nethercott, who Jimmy Seed had once considered a potential successor to Sam, was reserve.

When Sam took over at Luton Town, he and Helen moved house to Harpenden in Hertfordshire, an easy commute to and from Kenilworth Road. Conveniently daughter Moira was already at boarding school in the county. Although resignation from Luton in the summer of 1962 meant he was out of football for the first time since 1934, living a short distance from London ensured that it wouldn't be for long.

Fortunately, during his later career at Charlton, Sam wrote 'Sam's Smiles', short chatty pieces for a national Sunday newspaper. Later longer features were commissioned in which he humorously relived some of the amusing moments from

Somehow I dragged through that season and the winter that followed. No other doping chance came along and I decided to chance everything on a

Bitches often worry if the puppies are removed, but a good compromise is to have a second basket beside the one in which she lies. Keep it warm and then gently transfer the puppies there as soon as the mother has licked them clean.

SAM'S SMILES . . .

SHAN'T forget the last time York City reached a big Cup semi-final! I was playing for them – against Sheffield Wednesday at Hillsborough, the ground on which they play next Saturday – in the semi-finals of the North-South War Cup.

I dribbled the ball out from my own goal area—right up into Wednesday's penalty area. And there I lost it.

"Tony" Masserella, Wednesday outside-right, got possession—and set off for our open goal. Me after him.

Unfortunately, it was like a carthorse trying to catch a Lincoln winner—and I was the carthorse. Tony left me yards behind....

But then Tony shot. And his shooting wasn't half so good as his running. He put the ball yards wide! Was I relieved!

Here's wishing you luck next Saturday, York. And I'm sure George Lee, West Bromwich Albion winger, playing against us at the Hawthorns, will be thinking of you, too.

For George was outside-left in your team that day I nearly spoilt the show!

SAM BARTRAM

Sam's Smiles.

his playing days. Now that he was no longer working in football, he was asked to write more material. This ultimately led to Sam being taken on the staff of the *People* as a sports reporter and columnist.

He was a good catch for Fleet Street. Well known and respected throughout the game, Sam had played for, or managed, teams against every club in the Football League. His knowledge of the game was extensive. Eight hundred games for Charlton and over 250 as manager in three divisions plus the experience of playing in Australia, South Africa, North and South America and all over Europe, was something to write about in itself.

Bartram the newspaper writer's responsibilities were twofold; match reporting on a Saturday for Sunday publication and research during the week for his regular Sunday column. He would visit the paper's London office part time but much of his work was at the grounds talking to players and managers after training and at home as a soccer 'sleuth' on the telephone.

Much of this midweek soccer detective work, seeking the elusive scoop for his Sunday readers, was necessarily a hush-hush affair. The Bartram household became the nerve centre of Operation Sam, in which code words, soft voices and a highly prized personal phone book all played their role in tracking exclusive news, before cards, highlighting possible stories, were shuffled into position to form the basis of the copy for next Sunday's edition.

Sam was as eager a student of the game now as ever he was before. *Match of the Day* was compulsory viewing late on Saturday and a pile of Sunday newspapers were delivered and studied thoroughly. This clearly was the next best thing to playing, keeping Sam at the hub of the game. He particularly enjoyed his weekday visits to grounds, mixing socially with the players and keeping himself up to date with news and gossip from the clubs.

On the domestic front Moira finished at school after 'A' levels and entered the legal profession. At first attached to a firm of solicitors, then later qualifying as a

Sam and Helen on holiday in California with Helen's sister Alice (known as Pam) and her husband Russell.

Sam with his brothers and sisters, Henry, Mary, Benny and Ellen.

solicitor herself. Sam was so proud of his daughter that when they attended social gatherings together, he would introduce her and follow up with, 'She's a solicitor, you know.' Moira emigrated to Canada in the 1970s where she practiced her profession and became a corporate lawyer for a large international company.

In 1975 Sam was invited back to Charlton for a special occasion. After redevelopment at the southern end of The Valley, Greenwich Council built two high-rise blocks of flats overlooking the ground. Appropriately, as they stood behind the goal he had defended with distinction for so long, Sam was asked to perform the topping out ceremony on the flats and open Sam Bartram Close, the access road to the new development, which had been named in his honour.

Sam continued on the sports staff of the *People* until his retirement in 1979. Thereafter he continued to work for the paper as a freelance reporter. As one of their fraternity it was quite natural that he would take a particular notice of goalkeepers during matches he was covering. At Luton in April 1980, an incredible display by the visiting Shrewsbury 'keeper Bob Wardle in a 0-0 draw against promotion-chasing Luton earned the supreme accolade from Sam in his match report – a perfect mark of 10.

The Shrewsbury Town *Meadow Memories* website tells the story. 'Instead of facing the likes of Brentford, Blackpool and Colchester, Shrewsbury were travelling to new destinations – home games against Chelsea and West Ham were becoming commonplace. Still finding their feet in the then Second Division, Shrewsbury turned up at Luton's Kenilworth Road, a team who were managed by old Town boy David Pleat and who were pushing for promotion to the First Division. Names like Mal Donaghy, Brian Stein and Ricky Hill may not mean much to younger readers, but when Luton became a force in the First Division two years

A goalkeeper remembers: a return to The Valley, November 1975.

IT'S RIGHT UP SAM'S STREET!

IN THE Greenwich area the name Sam Bartram is a well-known one. Now it has been recorded for posterity . . .

Sunday People sports columnist Sam has had a road named after him — Sam Bartram Close.

The street-sign will be in a new estate road near Charlton football ground.

Sam explained how he was chosen: 'I played football for Charlton for 22 years and eventually got a ground gate named after me as well,' he said.

Sam played at Wembley four times and took part in 800 games.

Sam was asked to go along and top up the last piece of concrete on his road, and now he is just waiting for its official opening . . . and for the people to move in.

Sam, who joined the Sunday People in 1963, now lives in Harpenden, but used to do a lot of soccer coaching for youth clubs in south-east London.

He said: 'I feel it is a great honour to have a road named after me. Now I am kept for posterity!'

STREET of fame for the People's Sam Bartram

From the *Sunday People*, November 1975.

later, these names rolled off the tongue to many a schoolboy like myself while kicking a ball around in a playground. They also had a player called Bob Hatton. He wasn't bad either, for he had scored 19 goals that season and David Moss tallied 26. Luton had firepower. Luton were at home, playing in the sunshine, gunning for promotion... but we had Bob Wardle. Bob, or "Elastic Bob" as he was dubbed by the Anglia TV commentator during the game, was marvellous.'

Brian Swain of the *Luton News* said, 'Sam Bartram, a former Luton manager who knew a thing or two about goalkeeping, sat spellbound and at the bottom of his *Sunday People* match report gave Wardle the maximum 10 mark for his performance, something never achieved by a goalkeeper before.'

Just over twelve months later, after nineteen years covering hundreds of games, Sam filed his last match report. Appropriately it was from the familiar surroundings of The Valley. The report conveyed good news, a 2-1 victory for Charlton over Gillingham and promotion from the Third Division. More significantly, Sam's old club was on the rise again.

In July, the same newspapers that years ago had for so long carried tales of Sam the hero brought the tragic news that Sam had collapsed and died near his Harpenden home while returning from a visit to his newspaper office in London. It was even more of a shock and more sudden than his departure from Charlton a quarter of a century before.

Among the immediate tributes were these from national and provincial papers. Bill Bawden, writing in the venerable evening daily the *Shields Gazette*, whose Saturday sports editions had reported on Sam's early career, said 'Instead of our usual weekly trip back to the happenings of twenty-five years ago, tonight, I feel, we must pay tribute to and remember one of the true greats in football from this part of the world, Sam Bartram. Sam collapsed and died last night in the south of England where he has lived for several years... Sam was dubbed "The best uncapped goalkeeper in England" and with good reason. Boldon claimed him for their own, though he was actually born in Simonside not a stone's throw from the old Simonside Hall football ground... He was never selected for England, which many maintain to this day was a tremendous shame for he certainly earned the right to at least one cap to crown a great career... In the files is a story of him being offered £250 to "throw" a match, but Sam reported the attempted bribe to manager Jimmy Seed and went on to play one of the best games of his life. Football will badly miss Sam. He was one of those colourful but gentlemanly characters the present game doesn't seem to breed anymore.'

Malcolm Huntington of the *York Evening Press* wrote, 'Sam Bartram will be remembered by many York City fans for his fearless and acrobatic goalkeeping, which would have brought him many England appearances had it not been for the consistency of Frank Swift. During the Second World War, he was a guest player with City for three years when stationed with the RAF near Harrogate. I used to watch Sam in every City home game from behind the goal with my father and he became my boyhood hero. He was renowned as a saver of penalties. Then, unusually for a goalkeeper, he became City's penalty taker. He was saying one day in the dressing room at Bootham Crescent that no player should ever miss a penalty. City's captain, Joe Wilson, replied, "All right Sammy boy, if you think it is that easy, you can be the penalty taker from now." And so he was – and what's more he never missed for City, starting his run in his own goalmouth and thundering the heavy leather ball into the roof of the net with terrific power.'

Mike Langley, Sportswriter of the Year writing in the *People*, in a feature headed 'King of 'Keepers' wrote, 'Sam Bartram never really needed a press ticket to report football for the *Sunday People* these last eighteen years. His famous face opened all doors and the most cantankerous of commissionaires would stand aside for the only man in Fleet Street with his own entrance to a League ground. Yet the Sam Bartram Gate at Charlton commemorates even more than 800 appearances for his only club. It recalls an era when trams rattled through South East London, carrying crowds of 50,000 to follow the team that reached the first two post-war FA Cup Finals.

'I've stood among them on the top-most slopes of The Valley, a height from which even the greatest names look little larger than Subbuteo footballers. There was one player, though, whom distance could not diminish – and his name was Sam Bartram, the 'keeper with the quiff and the smile. His renown and recognition persisted through a generation who never saw him play. Fathers and uncles had passed on the legend of a sandy-haired acrobat in a green roll-top, who never lost his enjoyment for the game or gratitude to it for pulling him out of the mines in County Durham.

'No-one plays 800 games for any team without being good at his business. And no goalkeeper could play 800 games in those days – the days of hard toe-caps, shoulder charging and heavy leather balls – without being tough. Sam was tough but not in any aggressive way. He was never sour about the lack of England recognition. "I was kept out by a better man," he told me. "The best I ever saw, Frank Swift, of Manchester City."

'He liked newspapermen – and we liked him.'

eight

AWAY AND HOME AGAIN

In 1985 there was more unthinkable news; Charlton were forced out of The Valley. There was talk of selling the ground for development and relocating to a new smaller site near Greenwich. In the meantime the Addicks set up temporary home at Selhurst Park, in a ground-sharing deal with Crystal Palace.

The Valley faithful were dismayed by events and Selhurst Park was an unpopular choice of home ground as access proved difficult for a significant proportion of the club's fan base. Those with long memories knew that Charlton had left The Valley once before only to return and the loyal majority hoped history would repeat itself. Behind the scenes negotiations were taking place with the London Borough of Greenwich with this is mind. All was not plain sailing.

A more radical approach was adopted with the formation of The Valley Party, set up to contest the 1990 local council election on a platform of restoring Charlton Athletic to The Valley. An election strategy was devised and only two 'friendly' council members went unopposed. The Valley Party's trump card was a brilliant election poster campaign.

One of these striking posters featured a giant image of a diving Sam Bartram in mid-air, cap on, turning the ball round a post and bearing the slogan: SAM BARTRAM CAN'T SAVE CHARLTON THIS TIME, BUT YOU CAN. It helped raise awareness and support to such a level that The Valley Party claimed an astonishing 10.9 per cent share of the vote and won a seat on Greenwich Council.

The eventual outcome was that planning permission was granted and Charlton were on their way back to Floyd Road. All other alternative proposals were scrapped and home games were switched from Selhurst Park to West Ham while the now-derelict former ground was redeveloped in anticipation of Charlton's return.

Once again Sam had played a blinder for the Addicks. His spirit had never left The Valley, even if Charlton had. Also, having played as a guest for both Crystal

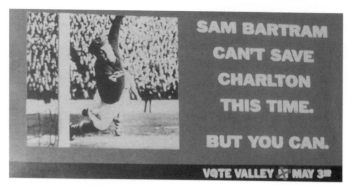

The Valley Party poster.

Palace and West Ham during the war, perhaps he was keeping an eye on the Addicks as they played there too.

In December 1992 it was back to The Valley. Appropriately, Portsmouth were the visitors for another of SE7's very special days. There was no cake on this occasion but after eight years in exile there was plenty to celebrate.

With Charlton safely re-established at The Valley, Sam's legacy remained undiminished. There was an overwhelming desire from many who remembered him and from others beguiled as youngsters by stories of this real-life hero regularly performing the seemingly impossible, to honour him at the rebuilt stadium. The Sam Bartram Entrance had been restored and incorporated into the new ground and Sam Bartram Close was another permanent feature close by, but once the Jimmy Seed Stand had been reopened there was a strong lobby for something similar in Sam's name.

'Make a Stand for Sam' was a headline that appeared in the national press. However with public safety now paramount at modern sports grounds, there is a preference for naming stands north, south, east and west for ease of identification by spectators, club officials, stewards and police. The supporters' club soon had an alternative idea, a statue.

Significantly, when Charlton Athletic established a committee to plan for the club's centenary in 2005, a Bartram statue was on the agenda. By a stroke of good timing the club was approached by a leading British sculptor, Blackheath-based Anthony Hawken, an ardent Charlton supporter. Early in 2004 it was announced that a statue was to be commissioned and would play a major part in Charlton's 100th birthday celebrations, subject to sufficient funds being raised. The cost for the project was £80,000, with the target for the public appeal set at £40,000. In May, The Sam Bartram Statue Fund was launched and despite the timing, at the start of the close season, the response was amazing.

Personal contributions, plus supporters' fundraising activities, kept the money coming in. BBC commentator and Sam Bartram fan John Motson donated his television notes for the home game with Southampton for auction and a bucket collection at the Centenary Match against Newcastle helped swell the proceeds. Meanwhile sculptor Anthony Hawken had started work. He was unhappy with his first design, a moving image of Sam running on to the pitch. It was replaced with a classic standing figure to contrast with the proposed background, the modern exterior of The Valley reception area.

Early in 2005 the Sam Bartram Statue Fund reached its target and with the club adding its promised 50 per cent share of the cost, work on completing the statue preceded apace and 9 June 2005, Charlton Athletic's 100th birthday, was the date set for the unveiling.

In the meantime unrelated images of Sam were popping up all over the place. In April 2004 he beamed out from The *South East London Guide* when the monthly magazine featured 'Super Sam', a colourful pop art work by local artist Cameron Walker, on its cover. Soon afterwards a 1950s portrait of Sam was spotted adorning Marshall Field's, the leading department store in Chicago, USA. It was not in the sports department but on display in another part of the building. In France, a large photograph of goalkeeper Bartram, crouching as if preparing to face a penalty, was seen on sale in a Paris photo shop window. The fact that he played in both Paris and Chicago for Charlton was surely pure coincidence.

During his playing days Sam was a magnet for youngsters. In those days of large crowds it was pay at the turnstiles, no need to book in advance like now. When the grounds were so full that it was difficult for small boys to see, they were often passed down over the heads of the crowd to a vantage point close to the pitch. Here they could almost touch their heroes. In made-up games in public parks, back alleys and school playgrounds, children would act out what they had seen. As the ball was produced and play was about to start, one of the participants would have said, 'You be so and so and I'll be Sam Bartram,' as he raced to take his spot between the coats or satchels that doubled for goalposts. This was where fantasy football began.

Some of these will have been the children who waited patiently at The Valley for Sam to appear after the match and proudly carry his boots up the road, as he set off on his journey home. At other times he was greeted in his local park with a cheery 'Hello Sam', from young folk as they passed by. Over fifty years on, the impromptu games may be long forgotten but the name Bartram still stirs emotions.

Thanks to an enterprising initiative by Charlton Athletic's community scheme, a whole new generation of children have been touched by Sam's exploits. Former schoolteacher and Charlton fan Peter Daniel devised a programme for local primary schools focussed on the Bartram legend. It told of Sam's life and to fit in with the National Curriculum was specifically built around the time of the Second World War. Ben Tegg and Natalie Evans, the club's community liaison specialists, made sure the ground-breaking project reached a wide group of

schools. Their efforts were well rewarded as hundreds of Greenwich schoolchildren fell under the Bartram spell.

At the same time Peter Daniel's story was adapted into a brilliant stage play by actors David Williams and Adam White. On 20 April 2005 the schools that took part in the project were invited to The Valley for the premier of *Bartram Saves the Day* performed by the Sub Rosa Theatre Group. The audience was so large that separate morning and afternoon performances were staged. It was a wonderful day. In the presence of Sam's daughter Moira, who was visiting from Canada, 500 schoolchildren interacted with football poet Crispin Thomas, Charlton's own artist and poet Ted Smith-Orr and watched the hour-long theatrical performance. They were also treated to meeting Peter Croker, a member of Charlton Athletic's 1947 cup-winning team, who specially brought his cup winners' medal to show the children.

This was high-octane stuff, a veritable Bartram special, all action and energy. The play featured the experiences of Charlton supporter Jimmy Thompkins, a Woolwich schoolboy, who is evacuated to Norfolk during the war. He relives the drama of Charlton's wartime and postwar Wembley cup finals and years later is given a ticket by his son – named Sam of course – to the 1998 Charlton *v.* Sunderland play-off final for a place in the Premier League. At the vital stage of the penalty shoot-out,

---

BARTRAM SAVES THE DAY – CHARACTERS AND CAST

Written by Adam White and David Williams from an original outline by Peter Daniel. Performed by the Sub Rosa Theatre Group for schools involved in the Charlton Athletic FC Sam Bartram Centenary Project at The Valley on Wednesday 20 April 2005 (twice) and to invited guests on the occasion of the Club's Centenary on Thursday 9 June 2005.

In order of appearance:

JIMMY THOMPKINS – David Williams
SARA, his daughter-in law – Marcella Kavanaugh
SAM, his son – Nick Austin
JACK – Phil Johnston
FINCHY – David Mann
CHARLIE – Patrick Halpin
VICTOR LYONS – Charles Jacobs
PAT – Aimee Thomas
FLORENCE – Kate Austin
JOYCE – Sheila McCabe
JEAN – Nina Baxter
HANK – Adam White
BBC Announcer [recorded] – Nick Austin

Jimmy calls for Sam to help Charlton goalkeeper Sasa Ilic, 'Sam, if you're listening… give the boy a hand.' When Ilic saves the penalty kick and the Addicks win, well-scripted and choreographed scenes of celebration follow and Jimmy looks up to the Wembley sky and says emotionally, 'Thank you, Sam.'

A sentiment that all involved must have felt for being part of such a memorable day. After the children left, Charlton's Floyds Bar became a 'green room' for those who had taken part and the camaraderie was appropriately continued later at the Royal Oak in Charlton Lane, where Sam and his singing was once a feature of supporters' club gatherings.

The Sub Rosa Theatre Group and *Bartram Saves the Day* were so well received that plans were swiftly made to include a repeat performance as part of the forthcoming 100th birthday celebrations.

As the day for the unveiling of the Bartram statue drew near excitement grew, so much so that the Charlton Athletic website carried a picture of the hole in the ground excavated to accommodate it. The sculptor Anthony Hawken and the Bronze Age Foundry in Limehouse, where the work was cast, worked at top speed to ensure that the one-and-a-half-times-life-size replica was ready on time.

On Thursday 9 June supporters and guests gathered for the unveiling around the tall, flag-wrapped structure outside the main entrance to the Charlton Athletic offices. On a sunny afternoon anticipation mounted as from a specially erected dais Charlton director and Sam's former playing colleague Derek Ufton spoke warmly about the goalkeeper who had been part of Charlton's team for so long, despite a career interrupted by the war years. He mentioned his sense of humour and physical strength and how, in training, he would get players to shoot directly at him and then rebound the ball way past them off his powerful arms. Derek invited Billy Kiernan, a goal-scoring winger of the Bartram era, to join him on stage and emphasised his terrific value to the team. He then added, 'I had the tremendous privilege of being a friend of Sam's, and I still miss him greatly. Sammy personifies all that is good in Charlton. If we are supposed to be the nicest, friendliest club in the country, then he was the nicest, friendliest man in the world.'

Charlton manager Alan Curbishley added, 'The affection with which Sam Bartram is held within the club is phenomenal.' Sculptor Anthony Hawken described the statue as 'The most important project of my life.' Centenary chairman Steve Sutherland then introduced Sam's daughter Moira, who said emotionally. 'This man was the kindest, most gentle man you would ever want to meet. He was the man who always called me 'Pet' and he was a great man. Thank you so much for all that you have done. He would be so honoured. Thank you.'

Moira was then joined by children from the Bartram schools project, who, accompanied by the familiar strains of '*The Red, Red, Robin*', helped her pull the chord and the Charlton flag dropped to reveal the imposing nine-foot bronze statue. Sam is depicted in a standing position, holding an old-style football, with his familiar roll-neck sweater cleverly fashioned in green bronze and folded cap in

Above: Former Charlton players at the Sam Bartram statue unveiling, June 2005.

Right: Members of the Bartram family await the unveiling.

Moira Bartram presents a 'Sammy' to David Smith, Charlton supporter and a major contributor to the statue fund.

hand. A modest low plinth gives the statue an intimate feel, as well as maximum impact. The ball Sam holds is not grasped to his chest in defiance of opposing forwards, as it would be if he was cast in action. Instead, he appears to be offering it as he did to admirers in his nearby shop after inflating their footballs, or indeed to be inviting watching youngsters to join him in a game before training. This was also known to happen on the very area the statue now overlooks.

A large number of former Charlton players, including plenty from the Bartram era, were present and they proudly gathered in front of the statue for press and public photographs. Among them were such stalwarts of the distant past as Eric Lancelotte, Peter Croker, Cyril Hammond, Billy Kiernan, John Hewie, Les Fell and Charlie Hall. So many former goalkeepers were there to honour Sam that they merited a separate group photograph.

The Bartram family was also represented in numbers. High above the statue hung images of Sam, painted by local schoolchildren. Appropriately, at an upper window was the bust of Jimmy Seed, Charlton's manager throughout the Bartram years, and the coup de grace, shining in its showcase in the main entrance just a few feet away, was the Women's FA Cup. The trophy, won by Charlton for the first time in their centenary year, is a replica of the FA Cup, evoking even more memories of those great Seed and Bartram years.

While this was the football club's day of celebration, the supporters' club staged their centenary party three days later. A day-long schedule of activities began by travelling back a hundred years to the place where Charlton Athletic FC was founded. At the site of a fish and chip shop down by the river, close to the Thames Barrier, a clutch of red-shirted fans gathered. An official with a megaphone announced 'One of our special guests today is Charlton goalkeeper from the fifties Albert Uytenbogaardt.' A tall, bronzed, handsome, grey-haired figure waved a Charlton flag in acknowledgement of the applause and set off with the group as they symbolically carried a crossbar at break-neck speed across Woolwich Road and past the site of Pound Park, an early Charlton ground. After a tantalising halt outside the club's former Royal Oak headquarters in Charlton Lane, it was on to the more familiar surroundings of The Valley to continue the festivities.

Albert Uytenbogaardt was one of a string of goalkeepers employed by Charlton during Sam's long career. None of them ever ousted him from his spot as number one. He was never dropped, making the role of Bartram's understudy a thankless task. In the Addicks' three seasons of First Division football before the war Sam missed only one game. He was replaced by young Syd Hobbins, a product of local soccer.

In Sam's ten seasons after the war he was missing from the Charlton line-up on just fourteen occasions. In his absence the Bartram mantle was taken over once by Syd Hobbins, six times each by South African international Albert Uytenbogaardt and Eddie Marsh, signed from Erith & Belvedere, and once by Eric Gill. Long-serving Hobbins, who had a good run when Sam was unavailable during the war, moved to Millwall in 1946. Uytenbogaardt returned to South Africa in 1954 and Eric Gill was transferred to Brighton & Hove Albion a year earlier. Jim Sanders, who made several wartime appearances left for West Bromwich Albion in 1945, Eddie Marsh and newcomer Frank Reed were the only Bartram stand-ins to remain at the club after he retired.

Both Albert Uytenbogaardt and Eric Gill were among the many former Charlton goalkeepers at the unveiling of Sam's statue. The bronze likeness, however, represented more than the figure of a goalkeeper from half a century before; it celebrated the club's former talisman who had inspired colleagues and the thousands who watched him for over two generations. When Sam left Charlton in 1956 a beacon that had burned so brightly for so long ceased to glow. It was like the extinguishing of the Olympic flame at the conclusion of the Olympic Games. Something very special had come to an end. Within six months Jimmy Seed's long reign finished and after one more season in the First Division Charlton were relegated.

Stanley Matthews in his book *The Way It Was* says, 'Sam Bartram kept goal for Charlton for twenty-two years and 582 League games. He defied the stereotype of red-haired players because he was always cool, calm and collected during games. Jimmy Seed, the Charlton manager, was so used to putting Sam's name down first on the team sheet that he continued to do it for weeks after he'd left in 1956 to manage York City.'

In his preface to Sam's autobiography Jimmy Seed wrote, 'When, for the last time, he took the goalkeeper's gloves from his gnarled hands – rough-hewn in the service

Sam meets new signing Albert Uytenbogaardt in 1948.

Above left: From Everton *v.* Charlton programme, January 1956.

Above right: Sam reflects on a glittering career.

of Charlton – and hung up his worn and dilapidated cap, it gave me cause for reflection. I remembered his loyalty. No more faithful, constant and true-hearted man has played the game of football. His club spirit stands out as a monument to young players and as an example to many older ones. While Sam was colourful and, at times, spectacular, he had great singleness of purpose; he subordinated all things to his career and to the service of his club. His cheerfulness, geniality and decorum in the dressing room stand out as a hallmark of all that is required of a professional footballer.'

When Sam played at Everton shortly before retiring, the programme carried a heading 'Charlton Athletic with Sam Bartram at Goodison Today,' an indication of his status within the game. As president of the Addicks' supporters club, he doubled as Charlton's number one fan. What an enviable situation for any club – having your best supporter in goal when he also happens to be one of the top goalkeepers around!

Sam's wage when he retired was £18 per week. This doesn't sound much now but it was above the national average at the time, although footballers were by no means in the top income bracket. From fourteen-year-old miner to forty-two-year-old First Division footballer was a long journey and Sam enjoyed every minute of his time at The Valley. There is a 1970s tape in the BBC archive of an interview by John Motson, in which Sam produces his FA Cup winners' medal from a pocket and says, 'You can never be poor with one of these.' It was his pride and joy and Sam was Charlton's.

nine

REMEMBERING SAM

From the Author

As a schoolboy I had the great pleasure of meeting Sam. My father had been in the Home Guard during the war with one of the Charlton directors, who was headmaster of a primary school in Bexleyheath. Being aware of my interest in football – he would supply us with match tickets – I was invited to his school prize-giving as a guest to meet Sam, who was presenting the prizes. What an honour this was, just headmaster Major Wilkinson, Sam and myself in the head's study prior to the event. Sam was in his England blazer and talking about football, I can't imagine I said very much but I was very happy to be there.

The next time we spoke was at The Den two days after his last game for Charlton. Sam played in a testimonial match for Millwall's John Short. In the car park afterwards I asked if he was staying on as president of the supporters' club. He confirmed he was, for a while. The last time I saw him was in the late 1970s, when I was on the staff at Orient FC. Sam called into the ticket office to collect his press pass before reporting on a Second Division game. I can see him now, immaculately dressed with polished shoes, smart raincoat, shirt and tie.

There have been so many occasions while compiling this book that I wished I could turn back the clock to that Saturday afternoon and ask his view on some of the incidents in his remarkable career. Sam was a modest man. He let his actions do the talking.

As I trawled for stories from those who knew him, I quickly found he passed on very little information to colleagues, especially about those fascinating early years in the North-East. It became apparent that I needed to find Sam's daughter Moira. Early investigation revealed she had moved to North America but no-one I contacted had any knowledge of her whereabouts. Then I had a large stroke of luck. After surfing around the internet, I managed to trace her.

A few days later we spoke on the phone and Moira explained that she had lost contact with most friends and family in England. So it was a great delight to be able pass on news of the proposed Bartram statue. Three months later Moira kindly visited Britain, for the first time after a long absence, in order to help with the book and meet the sculptor working on the statue of her father. By a very fortunate coincidence her visit coincided with Charlton's centenary match with Newcastle.

When the club heard that Moira was coming to town, she was immediately invited as guest of honour. We met for the first time a few days prior to the match at a West End hotel to discuss plans for the book. I arrived soon after 10.30 a.m. and, having been interrupted by nobody at all, we were still talking at 11 p.m. It was a delightful day. Concerning the Sunday match, Derek Ufton advised Moira not to travel by road, so we met at her hotel and took the train to Charlton.

This was literally a trip down memory lane for Sam's daughter, who had not been to The Valley since her father's last game when she was just ten years old. As we crossed Church Lane and turned into Floyd Road, things had hardly changed since 1956. The same tall houses are on either side, then we went past what used to be Sam's sports shop. There is no shop front now but it is still easily recognisable. Continuing on, we passed the familiar terraced homes near the ground and The Valley Superstore, with its large image of Sam in Charlton's centenary kit and into the much-changed Valley.

The match programme announced 'Bartram back at The Valley' the Charlton website proclaimed 'Sammy junior jets in' and on arrival Moira was appropriately the focus of attention in the guest lounge, with Sam's former teammates Derek Ufton and Peter Croker among the genial hosts. Before the kick-off Moira was escorted onto the pitch by Derek Ufton and introduced to the crowd. She received a hero's welcome and was appropriately presented with a Charlton centenary goalkeeper's jersey, bearing 'Bartram No. 1,' on the back. The Valley may have changed but when Moira heard '*The Red, Red Robin*' begin to play, she knew she was back home.

As for the book, I have Moira to thank for many of the photographs and other material from Sam's personal archive. Some of the personal reminiscences that follow are the result of a request made on my behalf by that fine *Daily Telegraph* columnist Robert Philip's feature, 'Play it Again for Sam', published at the time of the Charlton *v.* Newcastle centenary match. The response to the article was spectacular.

A disappointment has been not finding any photographs of Sam playing at schoolboy or non-league level, despite extensive research in the North-East. His sister Ellen kept a scrapbook dating back to his school days but sadly it went missing in a house move a few years ago. In a final quest for missing material I retraced the journey Sam made when he joined Charlton back in 1934. Having travelled on the main line to Newcastle, I took the train to the old Boldon

Derek Ufton presents Moira Bartram with a
'Sammy' in recognition of her father being
voted the club's greatest goalkeeper in
Charlton's centenary poll, 2005.

Colliery station, now called Brockley Whins on the Tyne and Wear Metro. From
there I walked towards where Boldon Villa's – Boldon Community Association
nowadays – ground was shown on the local map.

I walked for almost a mile. There was no pavement, no streets, just open land
until, through fresh-leaved bushes, down below a neat little football ground came
into view. In the far corner of the pitch was a red changing block with Boldon
CA (The Villa) proudly painted on the housing of the water tank above the
building. Alongside was a more imposing stadium with floodlights and modern
clubhouse, the home of Jarrow Roofing FC. However, it was the former, more
rustic, venue that held the appeal later that spring afternoon, but first I set off to
see what I could of Boldon.

Some old colliery rows were in evidence but so also was an Asda Wal-Mart
superstore – the biggest I have seen anywhere and the size of an international
airport terminal. Nearby was a multi-screen cinema, McDonald's and a pizza
house, all on a new complex in the heart of the village, near the football grounds.
The colliery closed in 1982 and how Boldon has changed. There is little evidence
of the mining days. Even the brass band folded in 2004, just seven years short of
its centenary, but the football team plays on, exactly where they played all those
years ago.

I returned to The Villa to see the goalposts being erected and the Colliery
Welfare Ground prepared for an evening game. I sought out club vice-president
Tom Bainbridge, who had helped me with my research some months earlier.
He was repairing a barrier behind the goal. Despite arriving 'out of the blue',
I was made very welcome. I heard the colliery used to overlook the pitch and
the open parkland to the north, where dogs now exercised and children walked
from school, was the site of the mine workings. At the other end, where pigeon
lofts and leek beds once flanked the ground, were modern 1960s houses complete with conservatories. One hundred years of history was right here, where the
young Bartram performed as wing half, centre forward and goalkeeper.

The scene was so English. A table at the gate with a gateman collecting a
£2 entrance fee from a handful of regulars. Adjacent was a tiny tea bar with an

aroma of cooking – and for a long period no visiting team. By the geographical peculiarities of the Wearside League, Boldon were due to meet rivals from far-off Cumbria. The kick-off was scheduled for 6.30 p.m. Well after that time, there was no team and no news. It seemed modern communication had passed them by. The referee for the match spent some of his waiting time by being fitted for a cricket umpire's coat, in preparation for a game he was umpiring the following evening on the well-manicured cricket ground next door. Then, around 6.50 p.m, a group of cars arrived carrying the visiting team. They had set off on their 160-mile trip at 3.30 p.m. and been hopelessly delayed.

I was so busy chatting to the Boldon faithful that the eventual kick-off went unnoticed. The standard of football was good and when Villa took the lead, as time was pressing for the last train to London, I reluctantly said my goodbyes.

There was an invitation for pie and peas afterwards but perhaps some other time. Back home the next day, I checked the internet to find the match ended 2-2. They must have finished in the dark! Sometime later, I noticed a message from Boldon's Cumbrian visitors on the Wearside League website, thanking them for their hospitality that evening – and so say all of us. Presumably the pies and peas went down a treat.

No early photographs were unearthed but it was a rewarding visit to the Bartram heartland where coal was once king. It was here that the young Sam Bartram grew up dreaming of becoming a professional footballer. Throughout his years of working in the local pit he would have drawn inspiration from the rich seam of soccer talent previously produced by the Durham coalfield. It was therefore especially appropriate that when the region's last mine closed, at Monkwearmouth in 1993, the colliery site was transformed into the Stadium of Light, the new home of Sunderland FC.

Bartram the miner, the daredevil teenage player whom the father of Durham City's Bill Willmer remembered as 'energetic, brave, fearless and foolhardy' in North-East non-League football, later became one of the most enduring exponents of the art of goalkeeping in a golden age of English goalkeepers. In the days when fans stood close in behind the goals, Sam enjoyed his banter with spectators up and down the country. They loved him for it and he received a warm welcome at home and away. Sam was adored at The Valley and respected wherever he played. His 800 games for Charlton, plus representative honours and wartime appearances all over the country, mean he must have worn the 'keeper's jersey a thousand times or more.

If he was gracing the game today, Sam would be in demand by TV programmes such as *Question of Sport* and *Match of the Day* and his years of service and dedication would almost certainly have brought recognition in the Honours List. It seems incredible that it is fifty years since he retired but he has left an indelible mark on the football of his generation and on thousands who saw him play. The following personal memories of Sam collected especially for this biography help explain why.

In early March 2006 Charlton Athletic further honoured their favourite son. Fifty years on from his last game for the club 'Bartram's' bar and restaurant opened at The Valley. A restaurant and bar throughout the week and open for drinks on match days. See you there soon!

An Understudy's View

The first time I heard the name Sam Bartram was in 1947. I was working for the Tramway Company (our local transport system) in Cape Town, South Africa, as a junior ticket office clerk. One of my jobs was to hand out the ticket boxes, waybills (the ticket sales were recorded on the waybill) and a punch (to punch the tickets). These items were given to the conductors of the bus or trolleybus to collect the fares from the passengers.

One of the conductors was a Londoner who was born in Charlton and as a youngster was a programme seller at The Valley. His father helped on the ground staff at some time or other and was a fanatical Addicks supporter. His name was George Courtney. Every day when George picked up his box, he would tell me about his heroes like Jimmy Seed, Jimmy Trotter, Sam Bartram, Don Welsh, Peter Croker, Chris Duffy, Bert Johnson and others. That was the year that Charlton had won the cup. As you can imagine George had plenty to talk about.

In 1947 I was only seventeen and had just progressed from playing as a goalkeeper for the Tramway under-18 team to the first team in the major football league, winning the cup for finishing top of the league. The sports pages in the local Cape Town English and Afrikaans newspapers were full of the Tramway Football Club.

When the 1948 season started I was a regular first-team player and was fortunate to be selected to represent the Western Province football team (the equivalent to county) that played the other provinces in the Curry Cup tournament. That same year I received a phone call from Ken (Polly) Kirsten, (who was also playing in the local league for a team called Park Villa), to say that he was offered a trial with Charlton and that they were also interested in me as a goalkeeper. I had to contact the local scout, a Mr Priday, who worked for Thomas Cook the travel agents. At that stage Charlton already had Sid O'Linn and Dudley Forbes playing for them.

When I arrived at Charlton in October 1948 I was the fourth South African to be signed on. Before leaving for England, I had quite a lot of publicity in the papers. as I was reported to be seven feet four inches and 'The Giant South African' signing for Charlton. The media were quite disappointed to find that I was only six feet five inches. Nevertheless, even at that height, I was the tallest player in British football.

On arriving at Victoria station on 14 October, I was met by Sid and Polly with Charlton chairman Mr Stanley Gliksten's chauffeur-driven car and taken to The

Albert Uytenbogaardt and Sam
together again, June 2005.

Valley. Mr Gliksten had flown down from Durban to Cape Town when he was on
one of his many business trips and interviewed me in the office of Mr Priday.

At the interview Mr Gliksten asked me to stand up, show him my hands and
turn around. 'You will do,' he said. So I was reported to have been discovered by
Mr Stanley Gliksten. Arriving at The Valley with my suitcase I was introduced to
Jimmy Trotter, who asked me if I had a pair of boots in my case and immediately
showed me where I could get togged up for a game.

Jimmy Trotter was the trainer to the FA Team who were training at The Valley
on their way to the continent and Jimmy had organised a practice game. I must
have played reasonably well as the score was only FA 1 Charlton 0. I was walking
off the ground at the end of the game all covered with mud, when Jimmy Seed
called me into his office and signed me for the season. For me, at the age of eighteen, everything was happening so fast on my first day in England.

After the game I was introduced to the rest of the Charlton players. I think Sam
was a bit put out that Jimmy Seed was looking for a replacement to take over
from him. In the days that followed the media were at The Valley taking photos
and interviewing me. The whole experience brought a major adjustment in my
life. Firstly I was in digs with Polly, living with people I had to get to know. The
training was exhausting, as I had never done any running in my amateur days.

During the years I played at Charlton we trained at The Valley, running around the track at the edge of the pitch. Whenever we cut corners, groundsman Bert Chase would shout at us, 'GET OFF THE BLOODY FIELD!' Irrespective of where you played, all the players had to get fit under the watchful eye of Jimmy Trotter, doing stamina training, running around the running track, lap after lap. Only when Jimmy was satisfied we were fit enough did he concentrate on speed, short sprints and quickness off the mark.

After the running, which was exhausting, the goalkeepers would go into the goals, where the players would be given about ten balls and kick hell out of us, with sometimes five balls coming to you at a time. Besides Sam, Eddie Marsh was the other goalkeeper on the books; Eddie and I used to get into one goal and Sam the other.

At the time of my arrival Sam was already fourteen years at Charlton, a star and legend in his own right and the most senior player on the books. Sam could get away with things that we as youngsters would not dream of doing. In the dressing room and on the training field, whenever there was any mischief, Sam was always in the middle of it. He had a wonderful sense of humour.

As a goalkeeper we never had any specialised goalkeeping training, so whenever watching other 'keepers play, I tried to study their every move to try and improve my game. Sam was not typical of the normal run of goalkeepers of his day, he had a style of his own. For example he seldom caught a cross – he used to punch a lot. Goalkeepers in those days were not protected and if he caught the ball he could be bundled over by one or two of the opposition players.

Jimmy Seed was never happy with 'keepers punching the ball. He always said if you can get your fist to the ball you can get your hands on it and distribute the ball to one of your players and thus keep possession. If Sam punched too much in a game, Jimmy Seed would blow his top at half-time. Whenever Sam saved the ball and the opposition fell back in defence he would come to the edge of the penalty area and roll the ball on the ground and advance upfield to gain more distance. When challenged he would kick the ball upfield.

In those days other goalkeepers did not dare leave the penalty area, but Sam was Sam. He was unconventional and did his own thing and the crowd loved him for it. I remember one game when he took the ball upfield out of the penalty box and when challenged booted the ball. Unfortunately he kicked it to one of the opposition who immediately kicked the ball back towards the empty goal. Sam was running back to the goal but fortunately defender Jimmy Campbell got to the ball before it crossed the line and rescued the situation. Jimmy Seed had a few words to say at half-time!

For all Sam's unconventionality, he was a brilliant goalkeeper. There were few other 'keepers with his reflexes, especially for the snap shot in the penalty area, where he was like a cat getting to the ball. His reflexes were so sharp. It has been written many times that if Sam had been more conventional, he would have played for England on quite a few occasions. The England goalkeeper at that stage was Frank Swift and he too was a legend.

On one occasion when Sam was injured, he was invited to play in a mid-week benefit game for Tommy Brown at Leyton Orient. Tommy used to play for Charlton and Scotland before being transferred; all the stars of the day were invited. I was very surprised when Sam approached me to take his place. I was honoured to accept, as to play in the company of those international stars was more than I ever expected. There were players like Stanley Matthews, Nat Lofthouse, Trevor Ford, Ted Ditchburn and other top players of the moment. I was fortunate to play on the side of the great Stanley Matthews.

Before the game all the players, referee and linesmen, got together. Being a friendly benefit game with about 30,000 spectators, to give the crowd good value for money, with no heavy tackling and plenty of goals, a 4-4 draw was agreed on. With strong tacking outlawed, all I did in the game was throw the ball to Stanley Matthews, who was always coming back for it, and let him get on with what he did best, making monkeys out of the opposition. One time he dribbled his way through the whole team, even going around Ted Ditchburn the other goalkeeper and then standing on the ball in the goalmouth, not putting the ball over the goal line. He then started all over again dribbling past players. He was laughing so much he eventually had the ball taken away from him.

In the last minute of the game our side was winning by four goals to three and play was in our penalty area, when one of our defenders 'accidentally' handled the ball. A penalty was immediately awarded. Ted Ditchburn came running from his goal to take the kick, tripping over the centre spot to the amusement of the crowd. Then, as Ted kicked the ball, I dived to my left so that he had the entire goal to shoot at. Unfortunately, the ball hit me on the foot and was cleared. The game eventually ended with our team winning 4-3. The crowd and players all thoroughly enjoyed the Wednesday afternoon spectacle.

I have Sam to thank for that day. It was one of the highlights of my English football career, playing with all those famous internationals. That was the first time that I personally met Stanley Matthews, who I subsequently played with and against on several occasions. After he eventually retired from Stoke City he made several trips to South Africa sponsored by the oil companies and I am privileged to say Stan always made contact with me whenever he came to S.A.

After spending almost six years at Charlton as Sam's understudy, with his popularity with the supporters and his consistency in goal, although Jimmy Seed tried to assure me that he needed me to take over from Sam when he eventually retired; I weighed up my options and saw that my future did not lie in English football. In those days although we were well paid by normal standards, we could not make enough money from the game for eventual retirement. Even if I was lucky enough to play for another ten years, I would still have had to make my way outside of football in the commercial world in order to make ends meet.

I decided while I still had a few more years as a sportsman and was in the public eye to return to South Africa. With a sad heart in May 1954 I left The Valley. I made many friends, who I left behind. My stay at Charlton was a wonderful experience. We were like one happy family and even to this day my loyalty is still with Charlton and their supporters.

Albert Uytenbogaardt, Durbanville, Cape Town, South Africa, former Charlton player and colleague

Others Remember

No one knew Sam better than me, apart from Mrs Bartram! I was on the staff at The Valley when he arrived for a trial and was signed on because they had no one else. He was magnificent, the best goalkeeper I've ever seen. Usually goalkeepers specialised in positional play but Sam also dived around and put on a show, he did everything. He was not merely an inspiration to his Charlton colleagues, he was more than that.

Eric Lancelotte, former Charlton player and colleague

Sam played in the first Football League match I ever saw. My father was a Methodist Minister in Creek Road, Deptford, and took me to see Charlton play Chelsea in 1952. We lived at Lewisham at the time and I visited The Valley regularly until going away to boarding school four years later. He was a great character and spectacular, I recall Sam taking off his cap to head the ball clear! I was later given his autobiography as a Christmas present.

John Motson, London, BBC television commentator

My father took me to see my first game at The Valley just after the war; it was a 0-0 draw with Aston Villa. We stood at the front behind the covered goal and when Charlton ran out for their kick about before the game, Sam trotted cap in hand towards the goal. To my surprise he didn't stop but continued towards the crowd and leaned over the barrier and gave me a sweet! What a great memory. Despite rationing, I kept it as a souvenir.

Trevor Bartlett

Above: Derek Dooley.

Left: John Motson.

In the late 1930s and 1940s my sister and I were big fans of Charlton. It was our home team and we would stand on the terraces well wrapped up in our red and white scarves and woolly hats. Win or lose they were still our team and were never booed like players are today. Of course when Sam came out in his green jersey, a huge cheer would go up. He sure was a great favourite.

I met him personally when he came into the sweet shop on the parade in Shooters Hill Road, where I started to work in 1946. Of course, sweets, cigarettes and ice cream were still rationed, so were limited and a great treat. Quite a few of the players lived on the estate behind the shops. Sam used to come in with Don Welsh, the captain – he was another popular chap and full of mischief. He would sit on the counter and tease my manageress, while Sam and I would have a chat. Sam knew I supported Charlton and if he let too many goals in, which was not very often, he knew he was in for a bit of a telling off! He would open the door and just put his head in, to take the stick I would give him. I would say, 'Well Sam, what have you got to say for yourself?' and he would come in and say, 'sorry.' So I would add, 'Don't let it happen again' – and then we would have a laugh.

Once I started in the shop I could not go to The Valley so often, as I had to work. The sweet ration used to be just sixteen ounces per month, so the last couple of Saturdays it was fairly quiet regarding customers, and the manageress would let me have a half-day off. I was fortunate to get a ticket for the cup final at Wembley in 1947 when we played Burnley. What a super day that was, and when Duffy got the winning goal that was the icing on the cake. Sam was quite fearless in defending his goal and would run out to punch the ball away and scare us. So we'd shout, 'Get back in your goal Sam!' He was certainly loved by all his fans.

Irene Evans, Welling, Kent

It was my first appearance in the Sheffield Wednesday team that season and my second appearance in total. One of the incidents in that game was that Sam came out for one of the long balls into the penalty area and he got to the ball before I did. To my amazement he dribbled the ball past me before clearing down the field. Needless to say I drew a blank that game and we lost the match.

Derek Dooley, Sheffield, former Sheffield Wednesday centre forward

As a young lad aged nine, I wrote to Sam for his autograph. I received a handwritten reply from him suggesting that I did not want a printed sheet of signatures but originals and if I sent my book to him, he would help me. I bought a new book and sent it to Sam and a week or so later received my book back with the autograph of every player on the books, Jimmy Seed's and Jimmy Trotter's as well. Sadly my mother gave my books to another lad when I was away at sea, some years later.

A year or two on, after a few letters had been exchanged and a parcel of programmes received during an illness, I met Sam at Herne Bay Pier Pavilion, where the Charlton players were giving a display of head tennis. I asked Sid O'Linn for his autograph and Sam came up and offered his. When I said I already had it, he said, 'You must be Alan,' and much of the rest of the evening I spent with the players. The memory of Sam's kindness has remained with me always. I keep in touch with the club's results thanks to the internet. There is no way I could ever support another team after Sam's kindness.

Alan Jordan, Beijing, China

We were always Charlton supporters and attended every home match. One occasion we were driving out of the car park and noticed Sam Bartram, boots under his arm, walking home through the crowd. My father asked us four boys if we would like to meet Mr Bartram. He drew up alongside our idol and said, 'My sons would like to shake your hand Mr Bartram.' My father was always very courteous. Then Sam put his ginger head through the car window and shook hands all round. We probably didn't wash for a week. That was sixty-six years ago and I was nine at the time and the memory is still fresh!

The Rev. Roger J. Hall, Styvechale, Coventry, Warwicks

I was ten years old when Charlton played in the 1946 cup final against Derby County and it was clear from the newsreel and radio commentary that Charlton had only got through to extra time because of the exploits of Sam in goal and then, the following year, their victory against Burnley was again due to his performance. In those days I lived in Highbury, quite close to the Arsenal ground. I had ambitions to be a goalkeeper and found that, by taking a tram from Highbury Corner and changing at the Elephant & Castle, I could get from Highbury to The Valley in around two hours. So off I went at the beginning of the 1947/48 season to see my hero in the flesh.

I immediately fell in love with the friendly atmosphere in the crowd and could stand in the 'boys' area' (there were quite a few girls there but at that stage in life this was of no special interest to me) and watch Sam perform. Being so close we could also hear the colourful language when (as often happened) the creaky defence made another mistake.

Sam's early experience as a centre forward was evidenced by his propensity in times of frustration to dribble the ball well down field before kicking it forward – a precursor to today's footballing goalkeepers.

When I see today's players roaring out of the ground in their BMWs, it causes me to reflect on the way in which Sam made his way home from The Valley. At the end of a match many lads would wait outside the stand for Sam to emerge with his little 'boot bag' in his hand. He would then walk up to Charlton station followed by a string of youngsters, reminiscent of the Pied Piper. If you were lucky he would let you carry his bag and he often gave some of the smaller fans a piggy-back. This was a man who would put at least 10,000 extra fans through the gate whenever he played.

Sam was and remains my sporting hero and I feel privileged to have enjoyed the opportunity to see him at such close quarters.

Brien Martin, London

Just after the war I had heard all about this handsome heart-throb Sam Bartram the Charlton goalkeeper, so along with a group of work colleagues I went to The Valley for the one and only time to see him play. About eight of us girls took up our position as close to the pitch as possible. No goals were scored but that didn't matter, we were only there to see flame-haired Sam! To watch him jumping around was enjoyment enough.

Ivy Game, Essex

From 1948/49 when aged eleven, I have two distinct memories. Charlton were pressing against Newcastle with every player in the opposition half, when a defender hoofed the ball far up the left wing. Bobby Mitchell, I believe, chased after it while Jackie Milburn took off down the middle, chased by half the Charlton team.

Sam decides that he can get there before Mitchell but just fails. Mitchell skips around him and squares the ball to Milburn who puts his foot on it and waits for Sam who is rushing back from the touchline. He can't wait for long because the defenders had caught up by then. Sam had the last laugh because Charlton won 6-3.

Secondly, against Blackpool, I witnessed what I have always thought of as 'perfect football'. Stanley Matthews rounded Charlton left-back Frank Lock and hit a low cross to Stanley Mortensen who, running in, hit it first time, low, just inside the near post. Sam flung himself to his left and fingered it round the post. Banks, Shilton or Jennings have never made a finer save.

Above all, Sam was a genuine character. Where have they all gone?

Brian Downing

Sam – Sam the Man – as likely to be found on the right wing as in goal! Perhaps an exaggeration but Bartram never believed the penalty area was a prison.

A pal and I cycled to every London ground during one summer holiday to collect autographs. Although the traffic was much less than now, The Valley (and Crystal Palace) were quite daunting for thirteen or fourteen-year-olds from Haringey, North London. We set off for Charlton and arrived before the staff. Sam and two others were the first players to turn up. They chatted and then produced a ball and had a kick-about with us. It was absolute heaven for two schoolboys.

Tony Bodley, Hertford

I recall a penalty incident at The Valley when Stanley Matthews celebrated his forty-second birthday in February 1956. Ernie Taylor, who also came from the North-East, sent a spot kick past Bartram who, having been upset by something Taylor said, then set off in pursuit of him. It was a bad day for Charlton, heavy rain and a good gate despite that, as Matthews once again proved his point to the London public. I recall Bartram's ginger hair – big powerful frame – and a good goalkeeper with it.

Jimmy Armfield, Manchester, former Blackpool and England full-back and captain

Jimmy Armfield.

I remember as a thirteen-year-old in 1949 going to see my team Everton play Charlton at Goodison Park. After five minutes the Everton full-back passed the ball back to goalkeeper Ted Sagar (another 'great'). Unfortunately, Sagar had come too far out and the ball went over his head and into the net for an own goal.

For the next eighty-five minutes Everton had 'shots in' and the play was never out of the Charlton half. Sam Bartram saved everything that day. There were more 'miracle saves' in that one game than in a whole season. I can see one save as though it was yesterday. The ball was crossed into the Charlton penalty area and the Everton forward Eddie Wainwright hit it on the volley from about the penalty spot. The ball was going into the top corner like a rocket and the crowd roared 'goal'. Somehow, Bartram got his fingers to the ball and tipped it round the post. Charlton won 1-0.

In 1959 I was invited for trials by York City where Sam Bartram was manager. I still have the invitation postcard signed by the great man! I went for the trial and hoped to get the opportunity to remind him of his great game against Everton. However, when the opportunity arose I was too much in awe of the legend to do so.

John Henesy

I recall that when Bolton Wanderers played Charlton Athletic and ends were changed at the start of the match, the kick-off was usually held up while Sam and Stan Hanson, the Bolton 'keeper, exchanged greetings in the middle of the pitch.

I also recall Sam diving in the mud at Burnden Park to save a shot and making a mess of his shorts. The Charlton trainer brought out a fresh pair and Sam changed them in front of say 40,000 and showed his bottom.

A truly great goalkeeper and I feel privileged to have seen him play.

Geoff Frith

Sam was a great goalkeeper, one of the best. We never put many past him. I would pick him for my team. I think Charlton Athletic held him in high esteem for his services to the club.

Len Phillips, Portsmouth, former Portsmouth and England forward

I have fond memories of the great man. At the end of the 1940s I was eight, having been born and bred in Charlton. Sam had a little sports shop in Floyd Road. It was the days of the leather football with the big leather lace in. It was a bit of a job to inflate it if the ball had burst, so we used to go to Sam's shop and he would inflate it and lace it correctly for (then) sixpence (2.5p). He would chat to us and we would be spellbound and didn't know what to reply – the great goalkeeper actually spoke to us! So, what we used to do was to play with the ball for a bit and then let it down on purpose so we could go back to his shop and ask him to inflate it again and we then managed to chat with him. We didn't do it too often because even if we all clubbed together sixpence was a hefty sum to find in those days.

We used to go to all the home games – get there as the gates opened and go straight to the front – there was no crowd trouble and all the men in the crowd used to make sure that us kids could see OK. Happy days.

Michael Johnson, Somerset

Born in Wolverhampton in 1943 I am of course, even now, a Wolves supporter. I began attending home matches with my mother, elder sister, maternal grandfather and maternal youngest aunt, all avid fans, in the early 1950s. Behind the goalposts at the Cowshed End at Molineux was our recognised spot. God forbade anyone else standing there!

I can well remember Wolves playing Charlton in those years with, inevitably, Sam Bartram in goal. Sam's red hair was thinning a bit when I saw him but there was still plenty of coverage. At the other end was Wolves' Bert Williams. The comparison of Bert with Superman – all well turned out and his blonde hair slicked down – and Sam with Dan Dare – rugged chin etc, comes readily to mind. Sam had a robust approach to the game, not only in goal but in the field. He was renowned for his bursts from goal, up the field and into the opposition's half. I can see him now coming out of the Cowshed goal with the ball, taking it on this occasion up the left wing, dribbling past Wolves defenders and shooting; then, of course, having to hare back centre field, to his own goal. God, the manager and other players only know what was said in the dressing room afterwards although, as I recollect, this action, long before Schmeichel et al, was not an uncommon occurrence.

A.E. Allsop

I am sixty-five and although a lifetime Gillingham supporter had Sam as a boyhood hero. My father used to take me to The Valley and we stood on the bank opposite the main stand. My enduring and endearing memory of Sam involves Frank Swift. It was traditional for the mascot to run out with Sam but on a visit by Manchester City he ignored Sam and ran out with Frank. On the first occasion of Sam receiving the heavy old fashioned ball, he threw it all the way into the City half, only for Frank to throw the ball much further back into the Charlton penalty area. This 'insult' to Sam's prowess induced him into kicking it

Bert Trautmann.

directly from a goal kick into Frank's arms only for it to be returned over Sam's head for a goal kick at the Charlton end.

David Dodd, Medway, Kent

I remember seeing Sam playing for Harrogate Railway in the 1940s. I think he was in the forces stationed nearby and played at centre forward for Harrogate.

Dr Gordon Smith

Those early days were somewhat impoverished and peoples' clothing reflected this. At The Valley, when the Addicks came out, they looked splendid, their red and white contrasting with the drabness of the crowds on the terraces. Sam's woollen sweater was equally dramatic, a deep emerald green, with a roll collar tight up around his neck. He wore the same socks as the rest of the team (those changed a few times but for a long period were red and white hoops). His boots were always very brown and clean. His thick auburn hair was well kept and nicely cut and he simply shone with health. His cap was seldom used but I cannot ever recall having seen him wearing gloves – and in any case, certainly nothing like the bulky gloves of current-day goalkeepers. Sam had a great smile, showing strong white teeth, in a time when visiting the dentist was not commonplace.

It was Sam's sheer presence on the field that was so impressive. A very fine man and such a shame that he was not given the international recognition he so thoroughly deserved.

Ken Willis, Broadstairs, Kent

I saw goalkeepers Sam Bartram and Ted Sagar playing when I was a prisoner of war and never imagined I would later play against them. Sam was a very open minded man. I liked him from the time I met him.

Bert Trautmann, Spain, former Manchester City goalkeeper,
Player of the Year and member of FA Cup-winning team 1956

My father told me about the Birmingham City *v.* Charlton Athletic match at St Andrews on 16 February 1946 in League South, a sort of intermediate season between the wartime leagues and the resumption of normal competitions the following season. The Blues and Charlton were running neck and neck for the title and drew 56,615, Birmingham's biggest crowd of the season. Remarkable considering the war damage St Andrews suffered, it well exceeded the attendance for the local 'derby' with Aston Villa a month earlier.

Charlton were awarded a penalty. This was taken by Sam who, according to Dad, ran all the way from his own goalmouth and took the spot kick on the run. The ball hit the crossbar, dropped down and was caught by Gil Merrick, Blues' 'keeper, who found centre forward Wilson Jones with his clearance. By this time, as you can imagine, Sam was chasing back to his unguarded goal. However, it all ended in anticlimax as Jones fell over the ball! City won the match 1-0, which proved decisive, as they won the title by the narrowest of margins.

Robert Bradley

I think the year was 1951 and at that time I played for Blackpool, mainly as deputy for the then England centre forward, the great Stanley Mortensen. On this particular Saturday 'Morty' was injured and I was selected to play against Charlton at Bloomfield Road. We won 3-0 and unbelievably I scored all three goals (although a couple of Sunday papers credited one of them as an own goal, a slight deflection from centre half Derek Ufton).

One of my everlasting memories in football will always be of Sam Bartram, at the end of the game, walking off with me, his arm around me and saying and I quote, 'Son, no player has ever hat-tricked me before in the First Division. You played very well.' These words from one of my heroes will stay with me for ever. What a gentleman and sportsman Sam was.

Len Stephenson, Blackpool, Lancashire

Len Stephenson (right) scores the first goal of his hat-trick despite a packed Charlton goalmouth.

Sam would take my autograph album to away matches and get the opposing team to sign. I gave him the book on a Thursday and it was returned the following Monday. Sam was completely fearless, a great sportsman and genuine role model for the youngsters of the day. I well remember one occasion when he was knocked unconscious as he gathered the ball – the trainer took quite a few seconds before he could release it and get Sam stretchered off!

The only sad outcome of this trip down memory lane is that when I returned home after the war, I discovered that my treasured collection of Charlton programmes and the autograph album had disappeared. When I enquired about them, my mother said, 'Well, you did tell me to throw out all the junk from your room!!!!'

Although I only had contact with Sam Bartram for a short time, it was a pleasure and an honour to have known him.

Don Carrott

I was a student at St John's College, York from 1959, which coincided with Sam Bartram being manager of York City. I was recommended to the club and played a number of 'A' team games and once for the Reserves.

As a North-East lad I was brought up on the legend of Sam Bartram and was taken to see him play. You can imagine my 'thrill' when Sam would regularly come to the college to ask me to play. Ever the gentleman, he was always friendly regardless of the problems he may have been having with the first team.

At the end of the 1950s and the beginning of the 1960s the continental and Brazilian influence had encouraged goalkeepers to roll or throw the ball to defenders or midfield players to start attacking moves. The one coaching tip I remember from Sam was for the goalkeeper to kick the ball from hand as far as possible, thus making it a 50/50 ball. Many teams do this now – particularly towards the end of a game.

Dennis Hinds

As a schoolboy I went to watch a wartime match at Huddersfield Town, the club I supported. I remember this game particularly as I was with my father and went in the stand for the first and possibly only time. I remember Sam as a goalkeeper who really punched the ball clear but most of all for a missed penalty. We had heard that he took penalties for York City and duly they were awarded one. He came and took it, the shot was saved and we had the exciting and hilarious sight of him racing back to his goal as the ball was transferred at speed to the other end. He got there just in time.

John Sneezum, Eastleigh, Hants

The much-loved Sam Bartram was a favourite football personality when I was a lad. I saw him play several times and I can assure you he was a top-class goalie. The problem was he was a showman, always likely to do something unusual and surprising.

I remember in an important cup game (I think it was against Newcastle) he intercepted a move and instead of giving the ball to one of his own side, he typically dribbled he ball out towards the halfway line flag. He then lost it, chased after the opponent in possession and slide-tackled him and the ball into touch. As ever, the crowd roared 'cos they were used to it! I don't ever remember seeing any of his own side getting upset with him. He was a good player, with thighs like tree trunks and everybody's favourite.

Ron Storey

I was lucky enough to see this fantastic, competent, daring, eccentric entrepreneur of a 'keeper quite a lot before he hung up his flat 'at. I seem to remember a game at The Valley against Chelsea. Seamus O'Connell was centre forward for the Blues that day. Bartram collected a totally non-threatening ball, extravagantly waved the entire home team up field, some penetrating deep into Chelsea territory. Sam, in his sea-going roll-top pulley and voluminous shorts dropped the ball to his very large dubbined boots and began a sort of swanky dribble towards the centre line. There wasn't another Charlton player in his own half.

I remember this in slow motion because that was about the speed of it. The goalie was clearly enjoying his usual self-appointed mission, as was the crowd, but as he approached the halfway line, now and again veering to the left, or to the right, to get the ball back under control, it became increasingly clear that his colleagues were not totally enamoured and the spectators' anxiety began to rise as well. Exhortations ranging from 'Get rid of it Sam' to 'What the b———— hell do you think you're doing Sam?' building in shrill volume from all interested Charlton parties on and off the pitch.

This unique occasion was one where ten home players and fans and the entire visiting team and fans completely and utterly shared a common incredulity at the sheer cheek of this man called Sam. At last, at long last, he reached the centre circle. Seamus O'Connell had, all this time, been standing there on his own, expressionless, stock still, hands on hips, watching – one would imagine in total disbelief. The rest of the Chelsea team were (sort of) keeping one eye on the rest of the Charlton team, with each and every red and blue hypnotised as one by the drama unfolding in front and behind them.

Beautiful to watch between the sticks, Sam, on this occasion graceful as a cart-horse, shimmied one way, then the other. O'Connell still did not move. As Sam was level with the patiently waiting Chelsea centre forward, O'Connell at last moved – but not a lot. Bartram, with glory in sight, was now and without fuss ball-less. As this realisation dawned upon him, he turned, like an ocean-going cargo boat in distress, to chase the rapidly disappearing O'Connell.

The ball was in the net and the scorer well on his way back by the time the Addicks' goalie reached his long-deserted goal line. What might he have given that day for the presence of that legendary Chelsea fog? Fans, being fans, muttered a bit but it didn't last. Sam was their Sam, much loved, could do no wrong. Those of us who were lucky enough to see this ordinary yet extraordinary man in action all have our various memories. Any occasional deranged activity was always far outweighed by his sheer ability and skill, stopping, on a dismally wet day, a sodden, dubbined, leather ball that weighed a ton and felt like a cannonball, when hammered by the likes of Nat Lofthouse into his solar plexus but not into the net.

Above all Sam Bartram remains in all our hearts and minds because he was and always will be one of us.

Doug Morrison

Sam and opposing goalkeeper Frank Swift once had some fun with a referee. Sam had fielded a back pass and punted the ball upfield. The ref, who'd just run back to the Charlton penalty area, set off into the Manchester City half. The ball went straight to Frank Swift who gave a signal to Sam and punted it back. The ref., still trying to keep up with play, sprinted back to the Charlton end. Sam then punted the ball straight back to Swift, with the referee doing his best to follow. He'd just got back to the Man City end when Swift kicked it back to Sam. By the third time this happened the crowd had realised what was going on and were laughing and applauding the poor ref. He, though, had had enough but was just about able to blow his whistle to stop play! It was some time before he was fit to resume.

Another time, Sam had dived through a melee of boots and bodies and at full length had fisted the ball into touch for a throw-in. To Sam's dismay, his captain, Don Welsh, wasn't at all impressed and shouted at him, 'Next time catch the b——— ball!'

Keith Ferris, Maidstone, Kent

SAM BARTRAM PROFESSIONAL CAREER RECORD

SEASON APPEARANCES: FOOTBALL LEAGUE AND FA CUP

1934/35 (part)
18 Third Division (South)

1935/36
39 Second Division, 1 FA Cup

1936/37
42 First Division, 1 FA Cup

1937/38
41 First Division, 5 FA Cup

1938/39
42 First Division, 1 FA Cup

1939/40
3 First Division, 24 South Regional League★, Football League War Cup Guest Appearances: 2 Notts County

1940/41
Guest Appearances: 16 Liverpool, 5 Bournemouth & Boscombe Athletic

1941/42
9 London League★, 6 London War Cup, Guest Appearances: 2 Bournemouth & Boscombe Athletic, 1 Brentford, 2 Crystal Palace

1942/43
2 Football League (South)★, Guest Appearances: 1 Birmingham City, 1 Bradford City, 1 West Ham United, 22 York City

1943/44
4 Football League (South)★, 3 Football League (South) Cup★, Guest Appearances: 30 York City

1944/45
5 Football League (South)★, Guest Appearances: 1 Bradford City, 1 Crewe Alexandra, 2 Millwall, 23 York City

1945/46
41 Football League (South)★, 10 FA Cup

1946/47
41 First Division, 6 FA Cup

1947/48
42 First Division, 3 FA Cup

1948/49
41 First Division, 1 FA Cup

1949/50
42 First Division, 4 FA Cup

1950/51
37 First Division, 2 FA Cup

1951/52
41 First Division, 1 FA Cup

1952/53
38 First Division, 1 FA Cup

1953/54
40 First Division, 2 FA Cup

1954/55
42 First Division, 3 FA Cup

1955/56
33 First Division, 3 FA Cup

★wartime competition

FOOTBALL LEAGUE AND FA CUP CAREER RECORD BY OPPONENTS

FOOTBALL LEAGUE 579 Matches
Arsenal 26, Bolton Wanderers 26, Chelsea 26, Blackpool 25, Portsmouth 24, Sunderland 24, Wolverhampton Wanderers 24, Manchester United 23, Aston Villa 22, Preston North

End 22, Huddersfield Town 21, Liverpool 21, Middlesbrough 21, Everton 20, Derby County 19, Manchester City 19, Stoke City 19, Burnley 17, Newcastle United 17, West Bromwich Albion 16, Sheffield United 14, Tottenham Hotspur 14, Birmingham City 11, Grimsby Town 10, Sheffield Wednesday 10, Brentford 8, Fulham 8, Leeds United 8, Leicester City 8, Cardiff City 6, Blackburn Rovers 4, Luton Town 3, Barnsley 2, Bournemouth & Boscombe Athletic 2, Bradford City 2, Bradford Park Avenue 2, Bury 2, Coventry City 2, Doncaster Rovers 2, Hull City 2, Norwich City 2, Nottingham Forest 2, Port Vale 2, Southampton 2, Swansea Town 2, Watford 2, West Ham United 2, Aldershot 1, Brighton & Hove Albion 1, Bristol City 1, Bristol Rovers 1, Clapton Orient 1, Crystal Palace 1, Exeter City 1, Millwall 1, Newport County 1, Northampton Town 1, Plymouth Argyle 1, Queens Park Rangers 1, Southend 1

FA CUP 44 Matches
Cardiff City 4, Fulham 4, Aston Villa 3, Preston North End 3, Wolverhampton Wanderers 3, Blackpool 2, Brentford 2, Burnley 2, Newcastle United 2, Portsmouth 2, Rochdale 2, West Bromwich Albion 2, Arsenal 1, Blackburn Rovers 1, Bolton Wanderers 1, Burton Albion 1, Clapton Orient 1, Coventry City 1, Derby County 1, Hull City 1, Leeds United 1, Luton Town 1, Manchester United 1, Stockport County 1, Swindon Town 1

The above record does not include matches *v.* Stoke City, Leeds United and Manchester United at the start of the abandoned 1939/40 season.

Roy Ullyett cartoon from the *Daily Express*.

OTHER CHARLTON ATHLETIC GOALKEEPERS DURING SAM BARTRAM'S CAREER

League and Cup appearances

1934/35
Cliff Owen 2 FA Cup
Harry Wright 14 Third Division (South)

1935/36
Harry Wright 3 Second Division

1936/37
—

1937/38
Syd Hobbins 1 First Division

1938/39
—

1939/40
Syd Hobbins 7 South Regional League★, Guest Appearances: S. Hall (Clapton Orient) 3 South Regional League★, Frank Swift (Manchester City) 1 South Regional League★

1940/41
Syd Hobbins 18 Southern Regional League★, John Oakes 1 Southern Regional League★
1941/42
Syd Hobbins 18 London League★, 1 London War Cup, Jim Sanders 3 London League★

1942/43
Syd Hobbins 26 Football League (South)★, 8 Football League (South) Cup★

1943/44
Syd Hobbins 20 Football League (South)★, 3 Football League (South) Cup★, Jim Sanders 6 Football League (South)★, 3 Football League (South) Cup★

1944/45
Jim Sanders 25 Football League (South)★, 6 Football League (South) Cup★

1945/46
Jim Sanders 1 Football League (South)★

1946/47
Syd Hobbins 1 First Division

1947/48
–

1948/49
Albert Uytenbogaardt 1 First Division

1949/50
–

1950/51
Eddie Marsh 4 First Division, Albert Uytenbogaardt 1 First Division

1951/52
Eric Gill 1 First Division

1952/53
Albert Uytenbogaardt 4 First Division

1953/54
Eddie Marsh 2 First Division

1954/55
–

1955/56 (part)
Frank Reed 1 First Division

★wartime competition

SAM BARTRAM FOOTBALL LEAGUE HONOURS

1934/35 Third Division (South) Winners
1935/36 Second Division Runners–up
1936/37 First Division Runners–up

Cup Finals

15 April 1944 Chelsea 1 CHARLTON 3, 85,000 (Wembley)
7 April 1945 MILLWALL 0 Chelsea 2, 90,000 (Wembley)
27 April 1946 Derby County 4 CHARLTON ATHLETIC 1★, 98,215 (Wembley)
26 April 1947 CHARLTON 1 Burnley 0★, 98,215 (Wembley)

★after extra–time

International Appearances

17 June 1939 South Africa 0 ENGLAND XI 3 (Wanderers Ground, Johannesburg)
13 April 1940 ENGLAND 0 Wales 1 (Wembley)
8 February 1941 ENGLAND 2 Scotland 3 (Newcastle)
7 June 1941 Wales 2 ENGLAND 3 (Cardiff)
26 May 1951 Australia 1 ENGLAND XI 4 (Sydney Cricket Ground)
30 June 1951 Australia 0 ENGLAND XI 17 (Sydney Cricket Ground)
7 July 1951 Australia 1 ENGLAND XI 4 (Brisbane Cricket Ground)
14 July 1951 Australia 1 ENGLAND XI 6 (Sydney Showground)

England Trial Appearances

1937 Possibles 1 PROBABLES 1 (Everton)
1954 ENGLAND 2 Young England 1 (Highbury)

London FA Appearances

11 March 1953 LONDON 6 Berlin 1 (Highbury)
4 June 1953 Genoa 1 LONDON 2 (Genoa)
18 November 1953 Berlin 0 LONDON 4 (Berlin)

ENGLAND'S INTERNATIONAL GOALKEEPERS DURING SAM BARTRAM'S PROFESSIONAL CAREER

Sep 1934 Wales v. England (Cardiff)	Won 4–0	Harry Hibbs (Birmingham City)
Nov 1934 England v. Italy (Highbury)	Won 3–2	Frank Moss (Arsenal)
Feb 1935 England v. N. Ireland (Goodison Park)	Won 2–1	Harry Hibbs (Birmingham City)
Apr 1935 Scotland v. England (Glasgow)	Lost 0–2	Harry Hibbs (Birmingham City)
May 1935 Holland v. England (Amsterdam)	Won 1–0	Harry Hibbs (Birmingham City)
Oct 1935 N. Ireland v. England (Belfast)	Won 3–1	Ted Sagar (Everton)
Dec 1935 England v. Germany (White Hart Lane)	Won 3–0	Harry Hibbs (Birmingham City)
Feb 1936 England v. Wales (Wolverhampton)	Lost 1–2	Harry Hibbs (Birmingham City)
Apr 1936 England v. Scotland (Wembley)	Drew 1–1	Ted Sagar (Everton)
May 1936 Austria v. England (Vienna)	Lost 1–2	Ted Sagar (Everton)
May 1936 Belgium v. England (Brussels)	Lost 2–3	Ted Sagar (Everton)
Oct 1936 Wales v. England (Cardiff)	Lost 1–2	Harry Holdcroft (Preston North End)
Nov 1936 England v. N. Ireland (Stoke)	Won 3–1	Harry Holdcroft (Preston North End)
Dec 1936 England v. Hungary (Highbury)	Won 6–2	George Tweedy (Grimsby Town)
Apr 1937 Scotland v. England (Glasgow)	Won 3–1	Vic Woodley (Chelsea)
May 1937 Norway v. England (Oslo)	Won 6–0	Vic Woodley (Chelsea)
May 1937 Sweden v. England (Stockholm)	Won 4–0	Vic Woodley (Chelsea)
May 1937 Finland v. England (Helsinki)	Won 8–0	Vic Woodley (Chelsea)
Oct 1937 N. Ireland v. England (Belfast)	Won 5–1	Vic Woodley (Chelsea)
Nov 1937 England v. Wales (Middlesbrough)	Won 2–1	Vic Woodley (Chelsea)
Dec 1937 England v. Czechoslovakia (White Hart Lane)	Won 5–4	Vic Woodley (Chelsea)
Apr 1938 England v. Scotland (Wembley)	Lost 0–1	Vic Woodley (Chelsea)
May 1938 Germany v. England (Berlin)	Won 6–3	Vic Woodley (Chelsea)
May 1938 Switzerland v. England (Zurich)	Lost 1–2	Vic Woodley (Chelsea)
May 1938 France v. England (Paris)	Won 4–2	Vic Woodley (Chelsea)

Far left: Ted Sagar.

Left: Harry Holdcroft.

Opposite left: George Tweedy.

Opposite middle: Vic Woodley.

Opposite right: Frank Swift.

Oct 1938 Wales *v.* England (Cardiff)	Lost 2-4	Vic Woodley (Chelsea)
Oct 1938 England *v.* FIFA (Highbury)	Won 3-0	Vic Woodley (Chelsea)
Nov 1938 England *v.* Norway (Newcastle)	Won 4-0	Vic Woodley (Chelsea)
Nov 1938 England *v.* N. Ireland (Old Trafford)	Won 7-0	Vic Woodley (Chelsea)
Apr 1939 Scotland *v.* England (Glasgow)	Won 2-1	Vic Woodley (Chelsea)
May 1939 Italy *v.* England (Milan)	Drew 2-2	Vic Woodley (Chelsea)
May 1939 Yugoslavia *v.* England (Belgrade)	Lost 1-2	Vic Woodley (Chelsea)
May 1939 Romania *v.* England (Bucharest)	Won 2-0	Vic Woodley (Chelsea)
Sep 1946 N. Ireland *v.* England (Belfast)	Won 7-2	Frank Swift (Manchester City)
Sep 1946 Eire *v.* England (Dublin)	Won 1-0	Frank Swift (Manchester City)
Oct 1946 England *v.* Wales (Maine Road)	Won 3-0	Frank Swift (Manchester City)
Nov 1946 England *v.* Holland (Huddersfield)	Won 8-2	Frank Swift (Manchester City)
Apr 1947 England *v.* Scotland (Wembley)	Drew 1-1	Frank Swift (Manchester City)
May 1947 England *v.* France (Highbury)	Won 3-0	Frank Swift (Manchester City)
May 1947 Switzerland *v.* England (Zurich)	Lost 0-1	Frank Swift (Manchester City)
May 1947 Portugal *v.* England (Lisbon)	Won 10-0	Frank Swift (Manchester City)
Sep 1947 Belgium *v.* England (Brussels)	Won 5-2	Frank Swift (Manchester City)
Nov 1947 Wales *v.* England (Cardiff)	Won 3-0	Frank Swift (Manchester City)
Nov 1947 England *v.* N. Ireland (Goodison Park)	Drew 2-2	Frank Swift (Manchester City)
Nov 1947 England *v.* Sweden (Highbury)	Won 4-2	Frank Swift (Manchester City)
Apr 1948 Scotland *v.* England (Glasgow)	Won 2-0	Frank Swift (Manchester City)
May 1948 Italy *v.* England (Turin)	Won 4-0	Frank Swift (Manchester City)
Sep 1948 Denmark *v.* England (Copenhagen)	Drew 0-0	Frank Swift (Manchester City)
Oct 1948 N. Ireland *v.* England (Belfast)	Won 6-2	Frank Swift (Manchester City)

Nov 1948 England *v.* Wales (Villa Park)	Won 1-0	Frank Swift (Manchester City)
Dec 1948 England *v.* Sweden (Highbury)	Won 6-0	Ted Ditchburn (Tottenham Hotspur)
Apr 1949 England *v.* Scotland (Wembley)	Lost 1-3	Frank Swift (Manchester City)
May 1949 Sweden *v.* England (Stockholm)	Lost 1-3	Ted Ditchburn (Tottenham Hotspur)
May 1949 Norway *v.* England (Oslo)	Won 4-1	Frank Swift (Manchester City)
May 1949 France *v.* England (Paris)	Won 3-1	Bert Williams (Wolverhampton Wanderers)
Sep 1949 England *v.* Eire (Goodison Park)	Lost 0-2	Bert Williams (Wolverhampton Wanderers)
Oct 1949 Wales *v.* England (Cardiff)	Won 4-1	Bert Williams (Wolverhampton Wanderers)
Nov 1949 England *v.* N. Ireland (WCQ) (Maine Road)	Won 9-2	Bernard Stretten (Luton Town)
Nov 1949 England *v.* Italy (White Hart Lane)	Won 2-0	Bert Williams (Wolverhampton Wanderers)
Apr 1950 Scotland *v.* England (WCQ) (Glasgow)	Won 1-0	Bert Williams (Wolverhampton Wanderers)
May 1950 England *v.* Portugal (Luton)	Won 5-3	Bert Williams (Wolverhampton Wanderers)
May 1950 Belgium *v.* England (Brussels)	Won 4-1	Bert Williams (Wolverhampton Wanderers)
Jun 1950 Chile *v.* England (WCG) (Rio de Janeiro)	Won 2-0	Bert Williams (Wolverhampton Wanderers)
Jun 1950 England *v.* USA (WCG) (Belo Horizonte)	Lost 0-1	Bert Williams (Wolverhampton Wanderers)
Jul 1950 England *v.* Spain (WCG) (Rio de Janeiro)	Lost 0-1	Bert Williams (Wolverhampton Wanderers)

Ted Ditchburn.   Bert Williams.   Gil Merrick.

Oct 1950 N. Ireland *v.* England (Belfast)	Won 4-1	Bert Williams (Wolverhampton Wanderers)
Nov 1950 England *v.* Wales (Sunderland)	Won 4-2	Bert Williams (Wolverhampton Wanderers)
Nov 1950 England *v.* Yugoslavia (Highbury)	Drew 2-2	Bert Williams (Wolverhampton Wanderers)
Apr 1951 England *v.* Scotland (Wembley)	Lost 2-3	Bert Williams (Wolverhampton Wanderers)
May 1951 England *v.* Argentina (Wembley)	Won 2-1	Bert Williams (Wolverhampton Wanderers)
May 1951 England *v.* Portugal (Goodison Park)	Won 5-2	Bert Williams (Wolverhampton Wanderers)
Oct 1951 England *v.* France (Highbury)	Drew 2-2	Bert Williams (Wolverhampton Wanderers)
Oct 1951 England *v.* N. Ireland (Villa Park)	Won 2-0	Gil Merrick (Birmingham City)
Nov 1951 England *v.* Austria (Wembley)	Drew 2-2	Gil Merrick (Birmingham City)
Apr 1952 Scotland *v.* England (Glasgow)	Won 2-1	Gil Merrick (Birmingham City)
May 1952 Italy *v.* England (Florence)	Drew 1-1	Gil Merrick (Birmingham City)
May 1952 Austria *v.* England (Vienna)	Won 3-2	Gil Merrick (Birmingham City)
May 1952 Switzerland *v.* England (Zurich)	Won 3-0	Gil Merrick (Birmingham City)
Oct 1952 N. Ireland *v.* England (Belfast)	Drew 2-2	Gil Merrick (Birmingham City)
Nov 1952 England *v.* Wales (Wembley)	Won 5-2	Gil Merrick (Birmingham City)
Nov 1952 England *v.* Belgium (Wembley)	Won 5-0	Gil Merrick (Birmingham City)
Apr 1953 England *v.* Scotland (Wembley)	Drew 2-2	Gil Merrick (Birmingham City)
May 1953 Argentina *v.* England (Buenos Aires)	0-0 (Aban 23 mins)	Gil Merrick (Birmingham City)
May 1953 Chile *v.* England (Santiago)	Won 2-1	Gil Merrick (Birmingham City)
May 1953 Uruguay *v.* England (Montevideo)	Lost 1-2	Gil Merrick (Birmingham City)
Jun 1953 USA *v.* England (New York)	Won 6-3	Ted Ditchburn (Tottenham Hotspur)
Oct 1953 Wales *v.* England (WCQ) (Cardiff)	Won 4-1	Gil Merrick (Birmingham City)

Oct 1953 England *v.* Rest of Europe (Wembley) Drew 4-4 Gil Merrick (Birmingham City)

Nov 1953 England *v.* N.Ireland (WCQ)   Won 3-1   Gil Merrick (Birmingham City)
(Goodison Park)

Nov 1953 England *v.* Hungary (Wembley)   Lost 3-6   Gil Merrick (Birmingham City)

Apr 1954 Scotland *v.* England (WCQ)   Won 4-2   Gil Merrick (Birmingham City)
(Glasgow)

May 1954 Yugoslavia *v.* England (Belgrade) Lost 0-1   Gil Merrick (Birmingham City)

May 1954 Hungary *v.* England (Budapest)   Lost 1-7   Gil Merrick (Birmingham City)

Jun 1954 Belgium *v.* England (WCG) (Basle) Drew 4-4 Gil Merrick (Birmingham City)

Jun 1954 Sweden *v.* England (WCG) (Berne) Won 2-0   Gil Merrick (Birmingham City)

Jun 1954 England *v.* Uruguay (WCQF) (Basle) Lost 2-4 Gil Merrick (Birmingham City)

Oct 1954 N. Ireland *v.* England (Belfast)   Won 2-0   Ray Wood (Manchester United)

Nov 1954 England *v.* Wales (Wembley)   Won 3-2   Ray Wood (Manchester United)

Dec 1954 England *v.* Germany (Wembley)   Won 3-1   Bert Williams (Wolverhampton Wanderers)

Apr 1955 England *v.* Scotland (Wembley)   Won 7-2   Bert Williams (Wolverhampton Wanderers)

May 1955 France *v.* England (Paris)   Lost 0-1   Bert Williams (Wolverhampton Wanderers)

May 1955 Spain *v.* England (Madrid)   Drew 1-1   Bert Williams (Wolverhampton Wanderers)

May 1955 Portugal *v.* England (Oporto)   Lost 1-3   Bert Williams (Wolverhampton Wanderers)

Oct 1955 Denmark *v.* England (Copenhagen)   Won 5-1   Ron Baynham (Luton Town)

Oct 1955 Wales *v.* England (Cardiff)   Lost 1-2   Bert Williams (Wolverhampton Wanderers)

Nov 1955 England *v.* N. Ireland (Wembley) Won 3-0   Ron Baynham (Luton Town)

Nov 1955 England *v.* Spain (Wembley)   Won 4-1   Ron Baynham (Luton Town)

WCQ: World Cup qualifying round. WCG: World Cup Group Match. WCQF: World Cup quarter-final

ENGLAND GOALKEEPERS IN UNOFFICIAL WARTIME AND VICTORY INTERNATIONAL MATCHES 1939-1946

Nov 1939 Wales *v.* England (Cardiff)   Drew 1-1 Vic Woodley (Chelsea)

Nov 1939 Wales *v.* England (Wrexham)   Won 3-2   Frank Swift (Manchester City)

Dec 1939 England *v.* Scotland (Newcastle)   Won 2-1   Tom Swinburne (Newcastle United)

Apr 1940 England *v.* Wales (Wembley)   Lost 0-1   Sam Bartram (Charlton Athletic)

May 1940 Scotland *v.* England (Glasgow)   Drew 1-1 Vic Woodley (Chelsea)

Feb 1941 England *v.* Scotland (Newcastle)   Lost 2-3   Sam Bartram (Charlton Athletic)

Apr 1941 England *v.* Wales (Nottingham)   Won 4-1   John Mapson (Sunderland)

May 1941 Scotland *v.* England (Glasgow)   Won 3-1   Frank Swift (Manchester City)

Jun 1941 Wales *v.* England (Cardiff)   Won 3-2   Sam Bartram (Charlton Athletic)

Oct 1941 England *v.* Scotland (Wembley)   Won 2-0   George Marks (Arsenal)

Oct 1941 England *v.* Wales   Won 2-1   George Marks (Arsenal)
(St. Andrews Birmingham)

Far left: Ron Baynham.

Left: Harry Hibbs.

Jan 1942 England *v.* Scotland (Wembley) — Won 3-0 — George Marks (Arsenal)
Apr 1942 Scotland *v.* England (Glasgow) — Lost 4-5 — George Marks (Arsenal)
May 1942 Wales *v.* England (Cardiff) — Lost 0-1 — George Marks (Arsenal)
Oct 1942 England *v.* Scotland (Wembley) — Drew 0-0 — George Marks (Arsenal)
Oct 1942 England *v.* Wales (Wolverhampton) — Lost 1-2 — George Marks (Arsenal)
Feb 1943 England *v.* Wales (Wembley) — Won 5-3 — George Marks (Arsenal)
Apr 1943 Scotland *v.* England (Glasgow) — Won 4-0 — Frank Swift (Manchester City)
May 1943 Wales *v.* England (Cardiff) — Drew 1-1 — Frank Swift (Manchester City)
Sep 1943 England *v.* Wales (Wembley) — Won 8-3 — Alec Roxburgh (Blackpool)
Oct 1943 England *v.* Scotland (Maine Road) — Won 8-0 — Frank Swift (Manchester City)
Feb 1944 England *v.* Scotland (Wembley) — Won 6-2 — Ted Ditchburn (Tottenham Hotspur)
Apr 1944 Scotland *v.* England (Glasgow) — Won 3-2 — Frank Swift (Manchester City)
May 1944 Wales *v.* England (Cardiff) — Won 2-0 — Ted Ditchburn (Tottenham Hotspur)
Sep 1944 England *v.* Wales (Anfield) — Drew 2-2 — Frank Swift (Manchester City)
Oct 1944 England *v.* Scotland (Wembley) — Won 6-2 — Frank Swift (Manchester City)
Feb 1945 England *v.* Scotland (Villa Park) — Won 3-2 — Frank Swift (Manchester City)
Apr 1945 Scotland *v.* England (Glasgow) — Won 6-1 — Frank Swift (Manchester City)
May 1945 Wales *v.* England (Cardiff) — Won 3-2 — Bert Williams (Walsall)
May 1945 England *v.* France (Wembley) — Drew 2-2 — Bert Williams (Walsall)
Sep 1945 N.Ireland *v.* England (Belfast) — Won 1-0 — Frank Swift (Manchester City)
Oct 1945 England *v.* Wales (West Bromwich) — Lost 0-1 — Bert Williams (Wolverhampton Wanderers)
Jan 1946 England *v.* Belgium (Wembley) — Won 2-0 — Frank Swift (Manchester City)
Apr 1946 Scotland *v.* England (Glasgow) — Lost 0-1 — Frank Swift (Manchester City)
May 1946 England *v.* Switzerland (Stamford Bridge) — Won 4-1 — Frank Swift (Manchester City)
May 1946 France *v.* England (Paris) — Lost 1-2 — Bert Williams (Wolverhampton Wanderers)

SAM BARTRAM'S GREATEST ENGLAND TEAM

Harry Hibbs (Birmingham City)
Warney Cresswell (Sunderland, Everton)
Eddie Hapgood (Arsenal)
Cliff Britton (Everton)
Stan Cullis (Wolverhampton Wanderers)
Joe Mercer (Everton, Arsenal)
Stanley Matthews (Stoke City, Blackpool)
Raich Carter (Sunderland, Derby County, Hull City)
Ted Drake (Arsenal)
Jimmy Hagan (Sheffield United)
Cliff Bastin (Arsenal)

Harry Hibbs
Born Wilnecote near Tamworth. Joined Birmingham City from Tamworth Castle in 1924. From a family of goalkeepers. His father, uncle and cousin all who wore the 'keeper's jersey. Less that 5ft 10in tall with an uncanny sense of anticipation which made him a master of positioning and an automatic choice for England. First capped in November 1929. Retired 1940, later becoming manager of Walsall. Sam's goalkeeping idol.

Warney Cresswell
Born South Shields and played for his local club, and was already an international when he joined Sunderland in 1921. Moved to Everton five years later and won Second Division, First Division and FA Cup winners honours in the early 1930s. A cool and consistent defender whose expert timing made him a powerful kicker of the ball and renowned tackler. Later manager of Port Vale and Northampton Town.

Eddie Hapgood
Born Bristol. Moved from Kettering Town to Arsenal and developed into one of the country's finest full-backs and most successful club leaders. First played for England in 1933 and captained his country 21 times. A member of the Arsenal team that won five League Championships and two FA Cups in the 1930s. Later manager of Blackburn Rovers and Watford.

Cliff Britton
Discovered in 1926 by Bristol Rovers while playing Sunday school football. Transferred to Everton in 1930 and won his first England cap four years later. Everton carried off the FA Cup and twice won the League Championship during his time at the club. A wing half for club and country, he went on to manage Burnley, Preston, Everton and Hull City.

Stan Cullis
Born Ellesmere Port Cheshire. Originally an inside right who joined Wolves from his home-town club in 1934. Switched to centre half with great effect and became captain of the Midlands club aged twenty. Earned his first international call up in 1937/38 and soon took over as England skipper. Later was a successful and innovative Wolves manager who brought regular European club football to England with a series of much publicised floodlit matches at Molineux in the mid-1950s.

Warney Cresswell.

Eddie Hapgood.

Stan Cullis.

Joe Mercer.

Stanley Matthews.

Raich Carter.

Ted Drake.

Jimmy Hagan.

Cliff Bastin.

Joe Mercer
Also from Ellesmere Port. Played in the school team with Cullis. Joined Everton as a teenager. Began as a forward who was effective on both wings. Moved to wing half and was first capped by England in 1938. He was a member of Everton's championship-winning team in 1939 and moved to Arsenal in 1946. He led the Gunners to victory in the 1950 FA Cup final and played in their League title-clinching teams of 1948 and 1953. A successful manager at club level, he also had a spell in charge of the England team.

Stanley Matthews
Born in Stoke and joined his home-town club as an office boy. A wonderfully talented winger who gained his first call-up for England as a teenager in 1934. Fast and elusive with a shot in either foot, he tormented opposing defenders throughout his career. Moved to Blackpool after the Second World War for whom he made three FA Cup final appearances, eventually gaining a winners' medal in 1953. Returned to Stoke and played in the First Division at the age of fifty. The first footballer to be knighted and the first ever 'Footballer of the Year' and 'European Footballer of the Year'.

Raich Carter
A product of Sunderland Schoolboys' football, he joined his home-town club as a teenage inside forward and was a major influence in their League Championship and FA Cup winning teams of 1936 and 1937. Made his England debut in 1934. Later won the cup with Derby County in 1946. Also a fine athlete and cricketer for Derbyshire. Went on to manage Hull City and Leeds United.

Ted Drake
Joined Southampton in 1931 and moved to Arsenal three years later. A prolific goalscoring centre forward in Arsenal's all-conquering years of the 1930s. Made his England debut against Italy in 1934. Scored seven goals for Arsenal against Aston Villa in 1935. England hat-trick against Hungary in 1936. Went on to manage Reading and Chelsea, leading the latter to their first championship in 1955. Also a county cricketer with Hampshire.

Jimmy Hagan
A creative inside forward with an eye for goal who is considered Sheffield United's greatest ever player. Born in Washington, Co. Durham, he played for Liverpool and Derby County before moving to Bramall Lane in 1938. Spent almost twenty years at United and was capped for England in 1948. Entered management with West Bromwich Albion in 1963 and later led Benfica to three successive Portuguese championship wins.

Cliff Bastin
Born in Exeter and scored twice for the Grecians on his home debut in 1928, aged sixteen. Moved to Arsenal in 1929 and first played for England two years later. One of the leading players in Arsenal's outstanding team of the 1930s. Scorer of 150 League goals during nearly twenty years at Highbury. Shares with Ted Drake the distinction of being the club's highest scorer in an FA Cup tie, having scored four goals against Darwen in 1932.

SAM BARTRAM MANAGERIAL RECORD

YORK CITY 12 March 1956 to July 1960

Season/ Competition	Position	Played	Won	Drawn	Lost	Goals For	Goals Against	Points
1955/56 Third Division (North)	11th	13	6	2	5	26	19	14
1956/57 Third Division (North)	7th	46	21	20	15	75	61	52
1957/58 Third Division (North)	13th	46	17	12	17	68	76	46
1958/59 Fourth Division	3rd	46	21	18	7	73	52	60
1959/60 Third Division	21st	46	13	12	21	57	73	38
FA Cup	–	12	6	2	4	14	10	–

Total: Played 209, Won 84, Drawn 56, Lost 69, For 313, Against 291, Points 210

LUTON TOWN July 1960 to 14 June 1962

Season/ Competition	Position	Played	Won	Drawn	Lost	Goals For	Goals Against	Points
1960/61 Second Division	13th	42	15	9	18	71	79	39
1961/62 Second Division	13th	42	17	5	20	69	71	39
FA Cup	–	6	2	2	2	10	9	–
FL Cup	–	5	1	2	2	5	9	–

Total: Played 95, Won 35, Drawn 18, Lost 42, For 155, Against 168, Points 78

RECOMMENDED READING

Sam Bartram by Himself, Burke & Co. 1956

Soccer at War, Jack Rollin, Collins 1985, reissued by Headline 2005

Forgotten Caps: England Football Internationals of Two World Wars, Bryan Horsnell & Douglas Lamming, Yore Publications 1995

Home & Away with Charlton Athletic 1920-2004, Colin Cameron, Colin Cameron 2004

The Essential History of Charlton Athletic, Paul Clayton, WH Smith 2001

Charlton Athletic Valley of Tears, Valley of Joy, Richard Redden, News Broker Services 1993

Charlton Athletic FC, Anthony Bristowe, Convoy 1951

York City A Complete Record 1922-1990, David Batters, Breedon Books 1990

Citizens and Minstermen, Citizen Publications 1997

The Definitive Luton Town FC A Statistical History to 1997, Steve Bailey, Brian Ellis, Alan Shury & Tony Brown, Soccer Data 1997

Schools' Football in Sunderland 1893-1993: A Record and a Celebration, Ron Gormley & Aidan Tasker, Sunderland Schools' FA 1993

ACKNOWLEDGEMENTS

Tom Bainbridge, Boldon CA (The Villa) FC; Alan Matthews, North Shields FC; Allan Purvis, Easington Colliery FC; South Tyneside Central Library, Bill Willmer, Robert Wray, Sunderland City Library, Easington Colliery Library, Aidan Tasker, Sunderland Schools' FA; Janis Blower, *Shields Gazette*; Mike Amos, *Northern Echo*; Searchers Family History Group, Marion Muncey, Sir Bobby Robson, Durham County Record Office, Rob Mason, historian, Sunderland FC; Jack Rutherford; Martin Emmerson, BBC Radio Newcastle; *Evening Press*, York; Malcolm Huntington; David Batters, historian, York City FC; Mike Persen, BBC Sport; Robert Philip, *Daily Telegraph*; Kevin Mitchell, *The Observer*; Mike Langley, *Sunday People*; Kevin Impey, *News Shopper*; British Library Newspapers; Colm Kerrigan, historian, English Schools' FA; Ian Cartwright, Charlton Athletic FC; Mick Everett, Charlton Athletic FC; Colin Cameron, historian, Charlton Athletic FC; John Rooke, Charlton Athletic Former Players' Association; Les Fell; John Treleven, historian, AFC Bournemouth; Steve Done, historian, Liverpool FC; Luton Town FC, Burnley FC, Crystal Palace FC, Watford FC, the Football League, League Managers' Association, Professional Footballers' Association; David Fowkes, London FA; Anthony Hawken, Doug Morrison, Cameron Walker, Peter Daniel, Crispin Thomas, Jonathan Boast, Justin Dix, Derek Allen; British Embassy, Berlin; David Evans, Rodney Bartram, Peter Wilson, OzFootball Archive.